D1636665

THE OLD SETTLER

BY JOHN HENRY REDWOOD

★

★

DRAMATISTS
PLAY SERVICE
INC.

THE OLD SETTLER
Copyright © 1998, John Henry Redwood

All Rights Reserved

SPECIAL NOTE

Anyone receiving permission to produce THE OLD SETTLER is required to give credit to the Author as sole and exclusive Author of the Play on the title page of all programs distributed in connection with performances of the Play and in all instances in which the title of the Play appears for purposes of advertising, publicizing or otherwise exploiting the Play and/or a production thereof. The name of the Author must appear on a separate line, in which no other name appears, immediately beneath the title and in size of type equal to 50% of the size of the largest, most prominent letter used for the title of the Play. No person, firm, or entity may receive credit larger or more prominent than that accorded the Author. The following acknowledgment must appear on the title page in all programs distributed in connection with performances of the Play:

Originally produced by the McCarter Theatre Center
for the Performing Arts and the Long Wharf Theatre

SPECIAL NOTE ON SONGS AND RECORDINGS

For performances of copyrighted songs, arrangements, or recordings mentioned in this Play, the permission of the copyright owner(s) must be obtained. Other songs, arrangements, or recordings may be substituted provided permission from the copyright owner(s) of such songs, arrangements, or recordings is obtained; or songs, arrangements, or recordings in the public domain may be substituted.

For

John Henry Redwood II
January 8, 1912 – March 7, 1973

and

Mary Elizabeth Redwood
July 6, 1912 – October 4, 1992

Thank you both for LIFE
Thank you for LOVE

THE OLD SETTLER was produced by Long Wharf Theatre (Arvin Brown, Artistic Director) in New Haven, Connecticut, on March 4, 1997. It was directed by Walter Dallas; the set design was by Loren Sherman; the costume design was by David Murin; the lighting design was by Frances Aronson; and the production stage manager was William H. Lang. The cast was as follows:

ELIZABETH BORNY	Brenda Pressley
QUILLY MCGRATH	Myra Lucretia Taylor
HUSBAND WITHERSPOON	Tico Wells
LOU BESSIE PRESTON	Caroline Stefanie Clay

THE OLD SETTLER was originally produced by McCarter Theatre (Emily Mann, Artistic Director), in association with Long Wharf Theatre, in Princeton, New Jersey, on February 7, 1997. It was directed by Walter Dallas; the set design was by Loren Sherman; the costume design was by David Murin; the lighting design was by Frances Aronson; and the production stage manager was Cheryl Mintz. The cast was as follows:

ELIZABETH BORNY	Brenda Pressley
QUILLY MCGRATH	Myra Lucretia Taylor
HUSBAND WITHERSPOON	Tico Wells
LOU BESSIE PRESTON	Caroline Stefanie Clay

THE OLD SETTLER was produced by Primary Stages (Casey Childs, Artistic Director) in association with Eric Krebs and Anne Strickland Squadron, in New York City, on October 1, 1998. It was directed by Harold Scott; the set design was by Bob Phillips; the costume design was by Debra Stein; the lighting design was by Frances Aronson; the stage manager was Peter Lomuscio. The cast was as follows:

ELIZABETH BORNY	Leslie Uggams
QUILLY MCGRATH	Lyunda Gravátt
HUSBAND WITHERSPOON	Godfrey L. Simmons, Jr.
LOU BESSIE PRESTON	Rosalyn Coleman

ACKNOWLEDGMENT

THE OLD SETTLER was originally presented as a staged reading at the 1995 National Playwrights Conference, Lloyd Richards, Artistic Director, at the Eugene O'Neill Theater Center.

It also received staged readings at The Border Playwrights Project (Borderlands Theater), Tucson, Arizona, Barclay Goldsmith, Producing Director; and at The Frank Silvera Writer's Workshop, Garland Lee Thompson, Founding Executive Director.

The Ministry of Culture of the Russian Federation
Mikhail E. Shvydkoi, Deputy Minister

The Theater Union of Russia
Alexander Gelman
Olga Novikova
Rima Krechetova
Valentin Vakoulin

Gregory M. Nersesyan, ASTICO
Sergei Artsibachev, Rukovod-Direcktor, Teatr Na Pokrovke, Moscow
George C. White, President, Eugene O'Neill Theater Center
Mary F. McCabe, O'Neill/Russian Coordinator
Julie Pinchuk, Russian Coordinator

And a special thanks to:
Ellen Pinchuk, Interpreter, Translator and Friend
Tatiana Rodzinek, Interpreter/Translator
Maria Zezina, Interpreter/Translator
The Townspeople of Shelekova, Russia

CAST
(In Order of Appearance)

ELIZABETH (Bess) BORNY—Black woman, 55-years-old.

QUILLY McGRATH — Black woman, 53-years-old. Elizabeth's sister.

HUSBAND WITHERSPOON — Black man, 29-years-old. Elizabeth's roomer.

LOU BESSIE PRESTON (Charmaine) — Black woman, 29-years-old. Husband's love interest.

TIME
Late spring, 1943.

PLACE
All of the action takes place in the apartment of Elizabeth Borny, in Harlem, New York.

ACT ONE
Scene 1
Scene 2
Scene 3
Scene 4

ACT TWO
Scene 1
Scene 2
Scene 3
Scene 4

THE OLD SETTLER

ACT ONE

Scene 1

Time: Spring, 1943. Thursday, late afternoon.

Place: All scenes take place in a tenement apartment belonging to Elizabeth (Bess) Borny, in Harlem, New York.

At rise: We see a living room and kitchen. The furnishings are those found in a living room and kitchen appropriate for that period. Even though the furniture appears old and worn, the rooms are well kept and neat. There is a rocking chair standing by the window of the living room facing out towards Harlem Hospital, which is across the street. There are lots of pictures of family and friends on a table, as well as, knickknacks which can be seen on the walls and scattered throughout the room. A worn rug covers the living room floor. There is a radio on a table which is playing. The kitchen floor has a worn flowered linoleum. There is an opening from the living room to the kitchen; one leading up the hallway to the bedrooms and bathroom; a door leading to a spare room off the kitchen and a door which leads into the apartment from the outside. There is a mirror that hangs by the door. The apartment door opens and Elizabeth (Bess) Borny, a black woman of 55, enters leaving the door open. She is dressed in black with a black hat and veil. She is carrying a black pocketbook, black gloves and a paper plate of food covered with wax paper. Elizabeth crosses into the kitchen and puts the plate on top of the stove. She then crosses and turns off the radio. After a beat, another black woman, Quilly Mc-Grath, 53, enters laboriously, closing the door. She is wearing a white dress with a gold sash and some medals affixed to her

7

chest. On her head is a white fez with a gold emblem of a scepter on the front and a gold tassel. She is carrying a white pocketbook and white gloves and wearing gold shoes. Quilly stops in the doorway catching her breath.

QUILLY. Oh, Lord have mercy! Whew! Them stairs. Shoot!

ELIZABETH. You forgot to turn the radio off again, Quilly. *(Quilly crosses to a chair and sits.)*

QUILLY. I left it on so these robbers and rapists would think somebody's home. That's the way I did it in Brooklyn.

ELIZABETH. You ain't living in Brooklyn no more. I've got to pay the electric here.

QUILLY. Shoot! *(She picks up a hand fan from under an end table and begins to fan herself.)* Goodness, it's hot already. What we got to eat, Bess?

ELIZABETH. You're supposed to be cooking this week. What you asking me for? *(She enters from the kitchen.)*

QUILLY. If you cook tonight, I'll take two of your nights next week.

ELIZABETH. No you won't. You'll scheme and connive to get out of it just like you're doing now. Cooking all that food on Saturday and then we eat the same old leftovers all week long.

QUILLY. Shoot Bess, I'm tired. That's the God's honest truth.

ELIZABETH. I don't understand it. You're two years younger than I am and you act like you're five years older. *(She exits to the bedroom taking off her hat.)*

QUILLY. *(Calling offstage.)* Age ain't got nothing to do with it, shoot.

ELIZABETH. *(From offstage.)* You should be tired. Running around like a chicken with his head cut off trying to get to that funeral.

QUILLY. And you still made us late.

ELIZABETH. I'm in no rush to get to no funeral; mine or nobody else's.

QUILLY. I wanted to get a good seat.

ELIZABETH. There's no such thing as a good seat at a funeral, Quilly.

QUILLY. I wanted to get where I could see.

ELIZABETH. I'm surprised you didn't get one of them folding chairs and sit right up front next to the casket.

QUILLY. *(Ignoring Elizabeth.)* Did you see that dress they put on her? That was one ugly dress. *(Elizabeth reenters from the bedroom buttoning her house dress.)*

ELIZABETH. Her sister said that was her favorite dress. Said, her husband wanted to put her away in something she liked and wore when she was living …

QUILLY. It was ugly then too, shoot.

ELIZABETH. … so her sister picked out that dress.

QUILLY. Quiet as it's kept, that dress probably killed her. Then they put her in all that bright red lipstick! Now they know she was too dark for all that bright red lipstick. Shoot. She looked better when she was living.

ELIZABETH. You're supposed to, Quilly.

QUILLY. That sure is some way to spend eternity; in an ugly dress and bright red lipstick.

ELIZABETH. Quilly, will you please be quiet about that woman!

QUILLY. All I'm saying is, we're sisters, and I hope whichever one of us goes first, the other one does better by her than that poor woman was done by her husband and sister. That's all I'm saying, shoot. *(Pause.)* You think he's ever going to get married again.

ELIZABETH. The woman's not in the ground good, Quilly. He's got to let a decent amount of time pass.

QUILLY. What for? She ain't going to get no deader. *(She stands and begins pulling on her girdle.)* I sure hope they didn't put no girdle on her. She'll be pulling on that thing forever, shoot. *(Pause.)* You getting ready to cook.

ELIZABETH. I told you I wasn't cooking. I'm going to eat that dinner I brought back from the church. *(She exits to the kitchen and begins to eat.)*

QUILLY. See now, that ain't right. You went down there and got you a dinner and didn't get me one.

ELIZABETH. They ran out of food. I told you, I said, "Quilly, come on now, let's get us a dinner." But no, you wanted to sit there until the last minute waiting for them to close that coffin.

QUILLY.   It wasn't no such thing. I didn't want all them little snotty-nose kids, running around down there with their greasy hands, to touch my dress. I ain't got no money to be buying another white dress, shoot.

ELIZABETH.   You didn't have to wear that dress today, Quilly. You wasn't doing nothing but showing off.

QUILLY.   The Ladies of the Golden Scepter were....

ELIZABETH.   Don't nobody in that church know nothing about no Ladies of the Golden Scepter ... except you and Sister Wallace. You ain't been to a meeting since you moved back here from Brooklyn a month ago. Over fifty and you and her running around the church in some old ugly uniform looking like the Gold Dust Twins.

QUILLY.   Oh, you just jealous.

ELIZABETH.   All right, I'm jealous. But I tell you this, you opened your mouth about frying chicken for Sister Wallace and her children to take on the train when they go back down to Georgia for Mother's Day. Now, don't you fix it in your head to try and connive me into frying that chicken because that's my week to cook. She's your lodge sister.

QUILLY.   I ain't going to ask you nothing.

ELIZABETH.   I'm just saying. I know you, Quilly.

QUILLY.   I ain't studying you. *(Pause.)* I sure wish I had somebody to go to Singleton's restaurant and get me something to eat. I can't climb them stairs no more today ... not with this girdle on, shoot.

ELIZABETH.   Then take it off and stop complaining. *(Pause.)* Ain't no use you looking, Quilly. You ain't getting none of my pig feet. Now you go on and eat them leftovers you cooked for the whole week. *(The doorbell rings.)* Look and see who that is.

QUILLY.   Shoot. *(She crosses to the window and looks out. Calling.)* Who is it? *(Pause.)* Oh, it's you.... When you ring the bell, come out and stand on the sidewalk so we can see who....

ELIZABETH.   Who are you talking to like that?

QUILLY.   Your "roomer."

ELIZABETH.   Husband?

QUILLY.   Yeah, "Husband."

ELIZABETH.   Did you throw the key down to him?

QUILLY. I had to find out who it was first. How many times have we told him to come out and stand where we can see him after he rings the bell. He rings the bell then stands in the hallway. Now how are we supposed to know who we're throwing the key to if he stands in the hallway where nobody can see him? Shoot! What happened to the keys you gave him?

ELIZABETH. I don't know. Just throw him the key, Quilly.

QUILLY. *(Looking for the key.)* I don't know why you want to take in some strange man anyway.... *(She finds the key tied to a handkerchief.)* You don't know nothing about him.... *(She crosses to the window and throws the key out. She shouts out the window.)* Here! *(To Elizabeth.)* You don't know who you're letting into our house.... He could be a rapist or something.

ELIZABETH. Well, unless something is wrong with him, you and me don't have nothing to worry about.

QUILLY. I don't know what you're talking about. You better talk for yourself, shoot. *(Elizabeth stands in the doorway and talks as she eats.)*

ELIZABETH. He wrote to me a couple of times after we agreed about him renting the room ... and I wrote him back. He's a very nice, polite, young man. Now, I want you to try and be nice to him. We need the money.

QUILLY. Where's he going to get money from? He ain't got no job.

ELIZABETH. How's he going to get a job when he's only been up here for three days, Quilly?

QUILLY. Well, if he'd stop running all over Harlem looking for that woman every day, he might be able to find him a job. And why ain't he in the Army like a lot of young men his age? There's a war going on. You ever ask yourself that ... or him?

ELIZABETH. No, I never asked myself that ... or him. And if he wants me ... or you to know, he'll tell us. And as far as his money goes, as long as he gets it honest, it's none of our business where he gets it from.

QUILLY. Well, if it's none of our business where he gets it from, then we don't know where he gets it from, so we don't know if he gets it honest or not.

ELIZABETH. The man ain't going to be up here for ever,

Quilly. Just as soon as he finds his girlfriend, he's going back down home.

QUILLY. Yeah, that's what they all say until they get up here and it starts getting good to them. What's taking him so long to come upstairs?

ELIZABETH. Deacon Slater said that Husband came into some money from selling some of the land left to him after his mama passed on. Now, he's paid a month's rent in advance and Deacon Slater has spoken for him and that's enough for me.

QUILLY. Well, Deacon Slater don't have to live with him. That's all I've got to say, shoot. And you can't trust no gator-tail eating geechees no ways. And both of them from the same hometown too. And one geechee is up here looking for another geechee who ran away from.... What's the name of that place he comes from? *(There is a knock at the door.)*

ELIZABETH. *(Whispering.)* You just remember that his rent is helping us keep this apartment.

QUILLY. I don't want to have nothing to do with him. All I want him to do is stay out of my way. *(There is another knock at the door.)* We're coming! *(To Elizabeth.)* Well?... Open the door for your "roomer." *(Elizabeth puts her plate down on the kitchen table and crosses to the door, opening it. A young black man, Husband Witherspoon, 29, enters carrying two cardboard suitcases. One has a rope around it.)*

HUSBAND. Afternoon, Miss Elizabeth.... Afternoon, Mrs. Mc-Grath.

QUILLY. What's the name of that place you come from down in South Carolina?

ELIZABETH. Quilly!

HUSBAND. You mean, Frogmore?

QUILLY. Yeah! Frogmore! That's just what I mean! Frogmore, South Carolina!

ELIZABETH. Quilly!... How did you make out, Husband?

HUSBAND. You mean with Lou Bessie?

QUILLY. *(To herself.)* Lou Bessie. Lord have mercy.

ELIZABETH. Yes.

HUSBAND. I went by that restaurant again where Lou Bessie had been working. The lady there, that I had been asking about Lou Bessie ... I guess she felt sorry for me....

QUILLY. I don't blame her.

HUSBAND. Well, she finally told me that Lou Bessie was cleaning house out in some place called.... *(Putting down his suitcases, Husband takes a piece of paper from his pocket.)* Some place called, Great-Neck. You know where that's at, Miss Elizabeth?

ELIZABETH. Yeah. That's out there on Long Island somewhere.

HUSBAND. I figure maybe I'll try and go out there and see if I can find her. The woman gave me the address. *(Proudly.)* She said she had heard of me and that Lou Bessie used to talk about me all the time when she first got up here.

QUILLY. You ain't down there in big foot country. You better not go out there messing around in them white folks neighborhood unless you wearing a dress and carrying a shopping bag.

ELIZABETH. Did the lady in the restaurant give you a telephone number so you might call Lou Bessie?

HUSBAND. No, Ma'am.

ELIZABETH. Well see, you just can't go out there walking around in them white folks neighborhoods because if the police don't get you, a bunch of white men might. Now don't you go thinking that because you're up here in the north, it's any different than it is in the south. In some ways it's worse.

HUSBAND. Maybe you're right. I think I'll go back to that restaurant and see if that lady has a telephone number for where Lou Bessie works.

QUILLY. Before you go, where's the set of keys Miss Elizabeth gave you?

HUSBAND. Oh ... I'm sorry, Mrs. McGrath ... Miss Elizabeth ... but I kind of lost them.

QUILLY. Oh, Lord. You can't go around losing keys. They cost money. And what if a rapist found....

ELIZABETH. That's okay, Husband. I got another set you can have.

HUSBAND. Thank you very kindly, Miss Elizabeth. I'll pay for them. It's just that, I ain't used to no keys. We never lock our doors down home. When I got to the front door with my bags, I went in my pocket looking for the keys and they were gone.... Oh, I forgot....

ELIZABETH. What's the matter?

HUSBAND. I left my other two bags with a man in the hallway to watch for me while I brought these suitcases up.

QUILLY. Are you crazy?

ELIZABETH. Go on back down there and get your bags, man.

HUSBAND. Yes, Ma'am. *(He rushes out of the door.)*

QUILLY. *(Calling after him.)* If he's still there! *(To Elizabeth.)* How stupid can one man be? I bet if he takes off his shoes, he still has chicken doody between his toes ... with his old country self.

ELIZABETH. Leave him be, Quilly. You forgot what you looked like when you first got up here. *(She crosses to the window and looks out.)*

QUILLY. I didn't look like that, shoot!

ELIZABETH. He's not there. Poor Husband is running up and down the street. *(Quilly crosses to the window and looks out.)*

QUILLY. Serves him right. Look at him. If he keeps it up, he's going to get hit by one of those cars.

ELIZABETH. Why are you so mean to him?

QUILLY. What you getting all upset about?

ELIZABETH. There's no reason for you to treat him like you're doing. He ain't done nothing to warrant that.

QUILLY. It ain't right that's why. You never even talked to me about taking in no roomer.

ELIZABETH. When I tried to talk to you about him, you wouldn't listen!

QUILLY. He was already here then!

ELIZABETH. Truth be known, I didn't have to talk to you about him at all. You wasn't even living here when I promised to rent the room to the man.

QUILLY. What's gotten into you, Bess? You were going to be living in this place all by yourself with some strange man?

ELIZABETH. People take in roomers to help with the rent all over Harlem and you know it.

QUILLY. But what Christian woman do you know living alone

14

in the same apartment with a man that's not her husband?

ELIZABETH.   Annie Mae Oxford who works down in....

QUILLY.   I said "Christian" woman! People down there at the church are all talking about.... *(The doorbell rings. Elizabeth looks out of the window.)* I bet he ran out of here without the key.

ELIZABETH.   *(Out the window.)* Who is it? *(Pause.)* After you ring the bell, Husband, don't stand in the hallway. Come out and stand where we can see who it is.

QUILLY.   I told you.

ELIZABETH.   Oh, shut up. *(Out the window.)* Just a minute, Husband. *(She looks around for the key.)*

QUILLY.   *(Pointing.)* Over there. *(Elizabeth crosses to Husband's suitcase and gets the key. She throws it out of the window.)*

ELIZABETH.   Here. *(To Quilly.)* I don't care what they're saying down there at the church. Ain't a body down there making my rent and it keeps going up. I was here by myself. When Mrs. Schivak moved to Florida, I lost three days work. That left me with only Mrs. Langbaum and that wasn't enough money. Even with him here, I'm still going to have to find more work. And you know with the war going on white folks ain't hiring help like they used to. Good, decent apartments, with all these rooms, are hard to come by.

QUILLY.   All I'm saying is, why couldn't you have gotten a woman roomer?

ELIZABETH.   Because I would rather have someone here that's been spoken for. When Deacon Slater asked if I'd be willing to take in a roomer, he said Husband was a very upstanding young man. And I could tell that from his letters. Now, I'd rather have him here than some fast, floozy of a woman I don't know. *(There is a knock at the door. Elizabeth crosses to the door and opens it. Husband enters.)*

HUSBAND.   *(Amazed.)* He's gone. I couldn't find him.

ELIZABETH.   Did you have anything important in the suitcases?

HUSBAND.   No, Ma'am.... Well, I did have a present for Lou Bessie ... and some canned peaches, canned succotash, canned stewed tomatoes and canned pickled watermelon rinds.

QUILLY.   All that in two suitcases? Well, he's sure going to eat good. You been up here for three days, why are you just getting your bags today?

HUSBAND. I went to that train station ... to that place where they hold the suitcases....

QUILLY. Baggage room.

HUSBAND. Yes, Ma'am. Pop Slater ... I mean Deacon Slater ... went with me to keep me from getting lost, but they had lost my bags. So they gave me a telephone number and I kept calling until yesterday when they said they had found them.

QUILLY. I bet when they found out you were colored, they didn't look all that hard.

HUSBAND. After I found out they had my bags, I tried to ride the subway down to that Penn Station by myself, but I kind of made a mistake. I kind of got lost. I did like Pop Slater told me. He told me to remember the Duke Ellington song, "Take the 'A' Train," and he told me to add, get off at 34th Street. But I kind of missed it because I ended up getting off at a station called Kingston-Throop.

QUILLY. That's in Brooklyn around where I used to live.

HUSBAND. I was riding so long I thought I was going to end up back in Frogmore. *(Laugh.)* So when I finally got to the train station, the baggage room had closed. And this morning I was waiting at that restaurant for that lady to come to work so I could find out where Lou Bessie was working.

QUILLY. Lord have mercy! Let me go change out of this girdle ...

ELIZABETH. Quilly!

QUILLY. ... and see about getting me something to eat. *(She exits to her bedroom.)*

ELIZABETH. You all right?

HUSBAND. What do you mean?

ELIZABETH. If somebody stole my suitcases, I certainly would be mad.

HUSBAND. It wasn't nothing much in them, so I ain't too bothered. I'll buy Lou Bessie another present. I might even take her and let her pick out her own present. But between you and me ... now don't tell nobody, Miss Elizabeth ... but there was a jar of corn liquor for Deacon Slater.

16

ELIZABETH. *(Laugh.)* Hush! *(Pause.)* Would you mind me asking you something, Husband?

HUSBAND. No, Ma'am.

ELIZABETH. When was the last time you heard from Lou Bessie?

HUSBAND. *(Pause.)* It's been a while ... I never gave it a great deal of thought, but it's been a while.

ELIZABETH. A month?... two months?

HUSBAND. Well, now that you mention it, maybe eight months. She sent me a sympathy card when my Mama died. That's the last I've heard from her.

ELIZABETH. Well maybe.... *(Pause.)* Never mind.

HUSBAND. Miss Elizabeth. Anything you feel you have to say to me, you say it. You've been very nice to me since I've been up here in New York. So if I'm doing something wrong or you see me going down the wrong road, I'd appreciate it if you'd let me know. All right, Miss Elizabeth?

ELIZABETH. All right.... What will you do if you can't find Lou Bessie?

HUSBAND. *(Pause.)* I don't know. It ain't never entered my mind that I wouldn't find her. After Mama died it just come natural that I come looking for Lou Bessie. See, Lou Bessie wanted me to come up here with her, but I'm the only child my mama had and I didn't want to leave her. So, Lou Bessie left and told me when I felt I didn't need to be under my mama, to come looking for her. So when Mama died, I took care of all the business, quit my job and came up here to find and marry Lou Bessie.

ELIZABETH. Well, maybe you should give some thought to what you're going to do if you don't find her ... or maybe she might have changed.

HUSBAND. To be quite honest with you, Miss Elizabeth, I really never gave much consideration about what to do if I don't find Lou Bessie. I guess I'm just so set on finding her that that's all I think about.

ELIZABETH. You said you quit your job? For some reason I thought you farmed.

HUSBAND. Every now and then, to make a little extra piece

of money, I'd go out and pull tobacco or pick some cotton, but, no, Ma'am. I used to work in a saw mill until my mama passed. Then a cousin that's an undertaker wanted me to go into business with him with the money I got from selling some of the land Mama left me. Oh, he had big plans for my money. He said that in a couple of years we could open another funeral home in Beaufort or Charleston. So I worked with him for about three months and I figured out that that wasn't the kind of work that was agreeable to me.

ELIZABETH. Why's that?

HUSBAND. I figure that you've got to be a certain kind of person to be an undertaker. I mean, you got to be able to see people sad and crying all the time without it bothering you. *(Quilly enters changed into a house dress.)* See, it's not like selling clothes or something like that. When people buy them kinds of things from you … well, in most cases, they come to buy when they're happy and they're happier after they buy. They leave smiling. But when people come to do business with an undertaker, they come in sad and crying and after you sell them the service, they leave sad and crying.

QUILLY. And after they find out how much it cost, they really leave sad and crying.

HUSBAND. Yes, Ma'am. *(Back to Elizabeth.)* I just couldn't take seeing people sad like that all the time.

QUILLY. Well, they just can't be staying around up here stinking. Somebody's got to do it. Shoot.

HUSBAND. I know, Mrs. McGrath. That's what my cousin said. But, I found out real quick that that somebody wasn't me. When I sell somebody something I want them to walk away smiling, not with tears in their eyes. You understand what I'm talking about, don't you, Miss Elizabeth?

ELIZABETH. I understand.

HUSBAND. Yes, Ma'am. Well, I better run on back down to that restaurant and see if that lady has a telephone number for where Lou Bessie works. I guess while I'm there, I'll get me something to eat.

QUILLY. You can bring me something back to eat while you're there. Where you going?

HUSBAND.   Over to the Down Home Restaurant on 145th Street and St. Nicholas.

QUILLY.   Well, before you come back, go over to Singleton's Restaurant on Lenox and 136th Street and get me a chittling dinner with cornbread, collard greens, black-eyed peas and swamp seeds.

HUSBAND.   What's swamp seeds, Mrs. McGrath?

QUILLY.   You from down there in geechee country and you don't know what swamp seeds are?

ELIZABETH.   That's rice, Husband.

HUSBAND.   Oh.

QUILLY.   Now, you ask for Lucy and tell her it's for Miss Quilly. She know how to fix my plate. And tell her I want some fatback in the collard greens and black-eyed peas.

HUSBAND.   Yes, Ma'am. *(Silence.)*

QUILLY.   Oh, my money is in my pocketbook in the room. *(Sitting.)* I'm too tired to walk all the way back there. You go on ahead and I'll give you the money when you get back.

HUSBAND.   Yes, Ma'am. *(He opens the door to leave.)*

QUILLY.   And bring me two lemonades and some peach cobbler.

HUSBAND.   Yes, Ma'am. *(Elizabeth takes a set of keys from a table drawer.)*

ELIZABETH.   Here's another set of keys, Husband.

QUILLY.   And don't lose them. We don't want no rapist walking in here.

HUSBAND.   Yes, Ma'am. And like I said, I'll pay for them.

ELIZABETH.   It's all right, Husband. Just be careful.

QUILLY.   And tell Lucy I want some pot liquor if she's got any. And I want a couple of pieces of fried chicken … the last part over the fence. That's for later.

HUSBAND.   Yes, Ma'am. *(He exits.)*

ELIZABETH.   You're going to give that man back his money, Quilly!

QUILLY.   I will!

ELIZABETH.   I mean it, Quilly. I know you. You're always crying poor-mouth. You'll keep putting it off with one excuse after another until he forgets about it or just plain gives up.

QUILLY.   I said I'll pay him back, didn't I? Shoot. What you getting all hot about?

ELIZABETH.   Because you're wrong. There's too many people out there in the streets just waiting to take advantage of someone like him without him having to worry about the people he lives with.

QUILLY.   He don't have to worry about living with me, shoot. We shouldn't be living with no man noways. Got all the folks down there at the church talking about us living here with that boy.

ELIZABETH.   All what folks, Quilly?

QUILLY.   Folks, that's all!

ELIZABETH.   Well, when "folks" start paying my rent, I'll worry about what "folks" got to say. Besides, the only "folks" I believe is talking is "Quilly folks."

QUILLY.   That's a tale! Sister Flowers said that at the last meeting of the Virginia Club everybody was just talking about....

ELIZABETH.   Everybody nothing! Sister Flowers was just saying what she wanted to say. She ain't nothing but an old news box. People need to mind their own business. That man ain't bothering nobody.

QUILLY.   You sure done got sweet on that boy.

ELIZABETH.   You talking out of your head.

QUILLY.   I ain't. That's the way you're carrying on, shoot. He done touched one of your buttons. That's what it is.

ELIZABETH.   Why don't you just shut up all of that foolishness.

QUILLY.   You walking too far ahead of that boy in age. *(The doorbell rings.)* I bet that fool done lost those keys again. *(Elizabeth goes to the window and calls out.)*

ELIZABETH.   Who is it? *(The voice of Lou Bessie Preston [Charmaine] can be heard.)*

LOU BESSIE.   *(Offstage.)* I was told I could find Husband Witherspoon here.

ELIZABETH.   Who's looking for him?

LOU BESSIE.   *(Offstage.)* He's been looking for me. My name is Charmaine. We're from the same hometown.

ELIZABETH.   You go by any other name?

QUILLY. Who is it?

ELIZABETH. A woman looking for Husband.

QUILLY. Oh, it must be "wife."

ELIZABETH. *(Out the window.)* Just a minute, I'll throw you the key.

QUILLY. What you throwing her the key for? You don't know who that woman is! *(Elizabeth throws the key out of the window.)*

ELIZABETH. You don't have to worry, it ain't no rapist. That's Lou Bessie.

QUILLY. I ain't heard her say nothing about no Lou Bessie. I heard her say Charmaine.

ELIZABETH. You mark my word, that's Lou Bessie.

QUILLY. Look, if you don't care nothing about your behind, that's your behind, but I care about mine. I live here too, shoot.

ELIZABETH. I know what I'm doing, Quilly.

QUILLY. No you don't. Not when it comes to that boy you don't. *(There is a knock at the door. Elizabeth crosses and opens the door. A young black woman, Lou Bessie Preston [Charmaine], enters.)*

LOU BESSIE. Hi, I'm Charmaine. I know Husband told you my name was Lou Bessie, but I changed it. That's why I didn't answer when you asked if I went by another name. I didn't want to be shouting Lou Bessie all over for everybody to hear.

QUILLY. Thank the Lord. At least one of you got some sense.

ELIZABETH. Is that what you're going to ask your people to call you when you go back down to Frogmore?

LOU BESSIE. Go back down where? Uh, uh, I ain't thinking about going back down to no Frogmore. *(Melancholy.)* I do miss my daddy though. Maybe when I make enough money, I could send for him to come up and visit me. I know he won't stay because he didn't even want me to come. But, this is a new life. I'm in a new and exciting place. So, I figured I needed me a new and exciting name. You can't go running around Harlem with people calling you Lou Bessie …

QUILLY. Amen.

LOU BESSIE. … so I changed it. I'm planning to get Husband to change his name too.

QUILLY. Amen again.

ELIZABETH. Quilly! I'm Elizabeth Borny and this is my sister, Quilly McGrath.

LOU BESSIE. Pleased to make your acquaintance.

QUILLY. Likewise. Now give back the key.

LOU BESSIE. Oh, yeah. Sorry. *(She gives the key to Quilly. She then begins to move around inspecting the apartment.)* Oooo — this is a nice place! *(She notices pictures on a table.)* Oooo … look at all these pictures! *(She crosses to the pictures, picking up a few and looking at them. She eventually keeps one in her hand as she talks.)*

ELIZABETH. Husband went down to your old job to see if he could get the telephone number for where you work. He should be back in a little while, if you want to sit down and wait. I know he'd want you to. He's been running himself crazy looking for you.

QUILLY. And everybody else.

LOU BESSIE. *(Run on.)* I can't wait long. Tonight's "Kitchen Mechanics Night" at the Savoy Ballroom. I know Husband can't wait to see me. He's nuts about me. He used to follow me all over down home. Got on my nerves so bad sometimes! Kept after me to marry him. I wasn't going to marry nobody and get stuck down there in Frogmore … and him tied to his mama like he was…. Uh, uh, not me. I'm so glad to be up here in Harlem. I used to hear about Harlem all the time when I was a little girl and I knew when I was fourteen that as soon as I could, I was coming to Harlem! I ain't never seen so many colored people in one place in all my life. Parties, dances, shows, jazz, parades and music going on all the time…. Even preachers standing on ladders in the streets, preaching. And now Harlem is full of all those fine looking colored soldiers from Fort Dix. No siree, I wasn't going to marry nobody and miss this.

ELIZABETH. *(Speechless.)* Well…. Husband seems to have his heart set on getting together with you.

LOU BESSIE. Yeah, well, maybe now that he ain't tied to his mama, things might be different between him and me. We can maybe get us a place on Sugar Hill or even Striver's Row. Paul Robeson lives on Striver's Row, you know. Then if Husband goes into the Army, they will send some of his money home as an allotment….

ELIZABETH. There's a war going on. What if he gets killed … what then?

LOU BESSIE. He ain't got to worry. They ain't going to let no colored soldiers fight in the war. That's what's so good about it. He can go in the Army and they will pay him and give him one of those pretty uniforms and he ain't got to worry about getting killed. Now, with the allotment and whatever money he has from his mama, we can open up a combination beauty salon/barber shop … maybe right across the street from the Savoy Ballroom where there's a lot of traffic.

ELIZABETH. You do know white folks downtown are trying to close the Savoy down, don't you?

LOU BESSIE. Is that the truth. I ain't heard nothing about that. Why?

ELIZABETH. I hear tell over a hundred soldiers and sailors caught venereal diseases at the Savoy.

LOU BESSIE. You hush!

ELIZABETH. And I heard they arrested a pimp and three prostitutes there not too long ago.

QUILLY. That's old mule poot! I'll tell you what it is. Those white men couldn't hold their water when they found out their white women was up here dancing and having fun with Negro men. They don't mind chasing around after Negro women, but they sure don't want their women with colored men.

ELIZABETH. Quilly, you ain't doing nothing but talking some old foolishness!

QUILLY. Don't tell me! Sister Laidlaw down at the church told me this man named O'Leary, some kind of a commissioner or something, told the people running the Savoy to stop advertising in white newspapers, to stop hiring white bands and to stop the dancing between colored and whites … which means colored men and white women. Don't tell me I don't know what I'm talking about, shoot.

ELIZABETH. Sister Laidlaw's mouth ain't no Bible.

LOU BESSIE. Well, anyway, we can call the place, "Charmaine and Andre's Beauty Salon and Barber Shop."

QUILLY. Who's Andre?

LOU BESSIE. That's a new name for Husband. Andre! Maybe

Dax! Something that sounds like it's from overseas ... something French. *(Pause.)* Well, I've got to be going. I'm meeting some of my friends and we're all going to the Savoy together. Oh, that's right! I'm going to have to teach Andre how to Lindy-Hop....

ELIZABETH.   He hasn't changed his name yet.

LOU BESSIE.   Oh, he will. He'll do anything I tell him to do. If he gets good enough at the Lindy-Hop, we might become partners and enter the contest at the Savoy Ballroom.

ELIZABETH.   He's going to be real disappointed that you didn't wait for him.

LOU BESSIE.   He won't be disappointed when he see me. Tell Andre to meet me at the Savoy. Tell him he can't miss it if he walks straight up Lenox Avenue to a Hundred and....

ELIZABETH.   I know where the Savoy Ballroom is at!

LOU BESSIE.   *(Pause.)* Well ... I'm going to go.... *(She puts the picture back on the table, then notices another one, which she picks up.)* Ooo ... isn't this a handsome cat. *(To Elizabeth.)* Is this you with your husband ... when you was ... young?

QUILLY.   Uh ... that's me and my husband.

LOU BESSIE.   Where's he at?

QUILLY.   I don't know. We're not together.

LOU BESSIE.   Why not?

QUILLY.   Well, if it's any of your business, he got too frisky. So, two months ago I put his behind out. You know, like you put a dog out.

LOU BESSIE.   Too bad. You think you'll ever get married again?

QUILLY.   Not if I have to marry another man.

LOU BESSIE.   *(Laugh.)* That's funny! Well, anyway, I've got to be going. I'll be seeing you again. And don't forget to tell Andre. Oh, and don't tell him about me changing my name to Charmaine. I want it to be a surprise. Bye. *(She puts the picture back on the table and exits.)*

QUILLY.   *(Laughing.)* So, that's Lou Bessie. She sure look stink.

ELIZABETH.   How long has that picture been out there, Quilly?

QUILLY. What?... I just put it out there a couple of days ago.

ELIZABETH. *(Screaming.)* When?

QUILLY. Yesterday!

ELIZABETH. Why, Quilly?

QUILLY. I ... I just put it there with the rest of the family. I live here too. I have a....

ELIZABETH. You ain't been living back here a month good and you're already starting your mess. I ain't going to have it. *(She crosses to the table and picks up the picture. She then crosses to the window to throw it out.)*

QUILLY. Don't, Bess!... Don't! *(Elizabeth stops in mid-air. Quilly crosses to Elizabeth and takes the picture out of her hand.)*

ELIZABETH. *(Pause.)* After all I've done for you and after all you've done to me, you're going to show it off. If I ever see that picture outside of your room again, so help me God, I'll throw it out ... and you along with it. *(She exits as lights go to black.)*

END OF SCENE

Scene 2

Time: 2:25 A.M., the next morning (later that night).

We see Elizabeth sitting in the living room, in her rocking chair by the window. The room is dark. After a beat, Quilly enters from her bedroom. Noticing Elizabeth, Quilly turns on the lamp.

QUILLY. What are you doing up this time of the night ... and sitting in the dark?

ELIZABETH. I couldn't sleep. I just thought I'd sit up for a while.

QUILLY. In the dark?

ELIZABETH. I was watching the goings on over there in Harlem Hospital. It's only Thursday night and those doctors and nurses are as busy as anything, so you know what it's going to be like on the weekend. If you want to see what us colored folks do to each other, all you have to do is go to any emergency room any Friday or Saturday night.

QUILLY. Well, if that fool you got staying here keeps running around like a chicken with his head chopped off, looking for that woman, you're going to be sitting here watching them sew up his head one Friday or Saturday night.

ELIZABETH. Don't be talking like that. You'll put bad mouth on him. Did you give him back his money?

QUILLY. I ain't had time, shoot! As soon as he walked in here with my food, and you told him where Lou Bessie ... Charmaine ... or whatever her name is, was going to be, he ran out of here like somebody who hit the number for fifty dollars. Has he come back yet?

ELIZABETH. No.

QUILLY. It's two-thirty in the morning! I know he ain't going to be walking in here at all hours of the night. Shoot, I ain't like him. I got to get up in the mornings and go to work.

ELIZABETH. What are you doing up anyway?

QUILLY. I had to go to the bathroom. Now I'm going to get me a drink of water.

ELIZABETH. That's a tale. You don't want no water. You just came in here being nosy and looking for something to fuss about. You could have gotten some water when you was in the bathroom.

QUILLY. I do so want some water, but I ain't drinking no bathroom water, shoot.

ELIZABETH. It's the same water, Quilly!

QUILLY. No it ain't. That's water from the bathroom. *(Indicates kitchen.)* That's water from the kitchen. I drink water from the kitchen ... from the icebox.... *(The noise of a key is heard in the door lock. The door opens and Husband enters tipping. He sees Quilly.)*

HUSBAND. Oh.... How are you, Mrs. McGrath?

QUILLY. *(Sarcastically.)* Good morning. *(She exits to the kitchen.)*

HUSBAND. How you, Miss Elizabeth

ELIZABETH. I'm doing pretty well. Husband, it's very late....

HUSBAND. Yes, Miss Elizabeth, I know, and I'm sorry. You see, I met Lou Bessie at that Savoy Ballroom like you told me.

We stayed there a little while then she took me to all these different places. *(Quilly enters carrying a glass of water.)* Jimmy's Chicken Shack, La Moor Cher....

QUILLY. La Marr Cheri!

HUSBAND. Yes, Ma'am. The Renaissance Ballroom, and a place that had a big, round, wooden bar....

QUILLY. Small's Paradise.

HUSBAND. Yeah, that's it, Small's Paradise. You know all these places don't you, Mrs. McGrath? *(Pause.)* And at the bar of the Braddock Hotel behind the Apollo, we saw Butterbeans and Susie. And look ... *(Husband pulls a coupon from his pocket.)* I won a meal for two at a place called Whimpy's from the drawing at that Renaissance Ballroom ... first thing I've ever won in my life. Only thing is, you have to eat the meal the same night you win between two and six o'clock in the morning. We went everywhere and Lou Bessie introduced me to all these different people. Some of them had these funny names....

QUILLY. Look who's talking.

HUSBAND. Black Sammy, West Indian Archie, King Padmore, Detroit Red....

ELIZABETH. What's she doing knowing people like that?

HUSBAND. I don't know. Lou Bessie just introduced me to them.

ELIZABETH. You better keep away from those kind of people. Those are gangsters.

HUSBAND. Yes, Ma'am.

QUILLY. What name you go by now?

HUSBAND. What you mean, Mrs. McGrath?

QUILLY. Is your name still Husband or is it Andre?

ELIZABETH. Quilly!

HUSBAND. My name is Husband, Mrs. McGrath.

QUILLY. Well, Miss Lou Bessie ... I mean Miss Charmaine said that she was going to change your name to Andre.

ELIZABETH. Quilly!

HUSBAND. My mama named me Husband and that's what my name is! And ain't nobody changing nothing!

QUILLY. I see. Bess, we need to get a block of ice from the iceman tomorrow. Good night. *(She exits.)*

HUSBAND. *(Pause.)* I didn't mean to bad talk Mrs. McGrath.

ELIZABETH. I know.

HUSBAND. It's just that nothing about me was right for Lou Bessie. She didn't like my suit.... She didn't like my shirt.... She didn't like my shoes. She even complained about my hair.

ELIZABETH. What's wrong with your hair?

HUSBAND. I don't know. But she said she'll take care of it. She can take care of all she want, but I ain't changing my name.

ELIZABETH. I don't think you should.

HUSBAND. And I'm going to keep calling Lou Bessie, Lou Bessie.

ELIZABETH. Well, I think if a person feels that they need to change their name, then we should respect what they want to call themselves.

HUSBAND. Charmaine? I don't know no Charmaine. I thought I knew Lou Bessie, but I don't know this person walking around calling herself Charmaine.

ELIZABETH. Sometimes people change, Husband. Lou Bessie from Frogmore, South Carolina ain't going to be the same Lou Bessie in Harlem, or Charmaine in Harlem. Maybe when she changed her name, she started being what she always wanted to be.

HUSBAND. What's that?

ELIZABETH. I don't know. That's something you have to find out ... you and Charmaine.

HUSBAND. Well, all I know is, I ain't going to stay here.

ELIZABETH. Husband, you can move out any time you get ready.

HUSBAND. Oh, no, Miss Elizabeth, I ain't talking about your house. I'm talking about up here ... in New York.

ELIZABETH. I thought you had a good time tonight.

HUSBAND. I did. But my mama used to say, "there's more to life than a good time." I've been up here for almost four days looking for Lou Bessie and I've seen a lot. I don't think we were meant to live on top of one another like people do up here. When I woke up in the mornings, these past few days, I used to feel low and I couldn't figure out why. Then when I got on my knees this morning to say my prayers, I tried to look up to heaven, and that's when it came to me. There ain't no windows in that room! Now, I don't mean to be talking bad about your house, Miss Elizabeth. You keep a nice, clean, comfortable house just like my mama used to. But, I can't open my eyes and see the light of day ... see the sky. When you do look out of a window, you look into a wall or into somebody else's window. I don't hear no birds or crickets ... don't see a tree or lightning bugs. There's no place to take off your shoes and feel the grass and dirt on your bare feet. No, Miss Elizabeth, just as soon as Lou Bessie and me get things straightened out, we're going back down home just like I planned.

ELIZABETH.   You tell Lou Bessie that you're planning on going back down home?

HUSBAND.   I ain't had time. There was always somebody around us. But you understand what I'm talking about don't you, Miss Elizabeth ... I mean going back down home and all?

ELIZABETH.   I know what you're talking about. I've been thinking about it for a long time myself. Used to be, every time I'd go back down home to Halifax, North Carolina, I'd have a hard time bringing myself back up here.

HUSBAND.   You know what I remember most? We used to catch junebugs and tie a string around their leg and then let them fly....

ELIZABETH.   *(Laugh.)* You did that too? You people in South Carolina was just as bad as us in North Carolina.

HUSBAND.   *(Laugh.)* You used to do that too?

ELIZABETH.   Sure did. But let me tell you, I stopped that when I found out why you could always find them around the outhouse. I stopped messing with them then ... the old nasty things. *(Reminiscing.)* But you know when I miss it most? When I go to church ... especially at night. That's when the memories are the strongest. *(As to herself.)* Walking in the dark of night down Route 301 to prayer meeting at the First Baptist Church of Halifax. Carrying a kerosene lamp so we could look out for snakes. Way after a while, before we could even see the church, we could hear it. The voices ... the singing. Then as we would get closer, we could hear the thumping of the feet on the old wooden floor as the folks rocked side to side to the singing. We didn't have no organ or piano. All we had was a tambourine, our voices, our feet, our hands and our love for the King. That's what I remember most. Sends chills up and down my spine just thinking about it. *(Elizabeth rocks from side to side as she sings "Tear Your Kingdom Down."* Singing softly.)*

    Satan, we're gonna tear your kingdom down,
    Whoa ho, Satan, we're gonna tear your kingdom down,
    You've been building your kingdom,
    All across this land,
    Satan, we're gonna tear your kingdom down.

(Recognizing the song, Husband joins in.)

ELIZABETH and HUSBAND. *(Volume builds.)*

    Preacher's gonna preach your kingdom down,
    Whoa ho, Preacher's gonna preach your kingdom down,
    You've been building ...

QUILLY. *(Offstage.)* Will you all please be quite out there. I'm trying to get me some sleep. *(They stop singing. Silence.)*

ELIZABETH. It is late.

HUSBAND. Yes, Ma'am. Good night, Miss Elizabeth.

ELIZABETH. Good night. *(Husband begins to cross to the door.)* Husband. I'm glad you finally found Lou Bessie.

HUSBAND. Yes, Ma'am. *(Courageous.)* Uh ... Miss Elizabeth....

ELIZABETH. Yes?

HUSBAND. *(Pause.)* You think you might be hungry?

ELIZABETH. What?

HUSBAND. Well, I see you and Mrs. McGrath are still up.

ELIZABETH. Quilly got up to get some water and I couldn't sleep.

HUSBAND. When I couldn't sleep, Mama would say it was because something mighty strong was on my mind or my stomach was talking to me. You worried about something, Miss Elizabeth?

ELIZABETH. No, I ain't worried about nothing.

HUSBAND. Well then, your stomach must be talking to you. Now, I'm going to get me something to eat with this ticket I

* See Special Note on Songs and Recordings on copyright page.

30

won…. *(Pause.)* I was thinking that maybe you might like to go get something to eat with me. *(Pause.)* It's free.

ELIZABETH.   It's almost three o'clock in the morning, Husband.

HUSBAND.   The ticket is only good for tonight. And I can only use it between two and six o'clock in the morning. And like I said, it's the first thing I've ever won and I ain't going to let it go to waste.

ELIZABETH.   I've only been out of this house past eleven o'clock once a year for years and that was for "Watch Hour" service at the church on New Year's Eve to bring in the New Year. I don't even know what it looks like out there this time of the night.

HUSBAND.   I'm thinking that you don't have to go to work in the morning.

ELIZABETH.   Uh, no, Husband, thank you … but, … it's too late. Where's Lou Bessie? Why ain't you eating with her?

HUSBAND.   *(Hesitant.)* Well, I didn't want to say in front of Mrs. McGrath. You see, I don't know where Lou Bessie is. She left me sitting at a table in Jimmy's Chicken Shack and went off with these two soldiers and a woman. She told me she would be back in a few minutes then we would go and eat. I waited and waited but she didn't come back. Then some fellow that worked there told me I just couldn't sit there and not buy something. I don't drink, so I wasn't going to buy no liquor. I had already bought a bunch of drinks for Lou Bessie … and her friends. So, I went outside and waited some more, but she still didn't come back. So, I came home.

ELIZABETH.   I see.

HUSBAND.   I've been eating alone in restaurants since I've been up here. I figured when I found Lou Bessie, I wouldn't have to eat by myself no more. It's lonely eating by myself. Ever since my mama died I've been eating alone. *(Pause.)* I guess only somebody who's been lonely can understand being alone.

ELIZABETH.   *(Pause.)* I understand about eating alone … and being alone.

HUSBAND.   *(Pause.)* Well, if I keep running my mouth you ain't never going to get no sleep. *(He begins to cross to the door.)*

31

Good night, Miss Elizabeth. And I'll be quiet when I come in.

ELIZABETH. You still going out to eat at this time of the night?

HUSBAND. Yes, Ma'am. I'm still hungry, Lou Bessie or no Lou Bessie.

ELIZABETH. *(Pause.)* If you can wait a minute, I'll get dressed and go with you. That is, if you still want me to.

HUSBAND. Oh, yes, Ma'am! I can wait. *(Elizabeth begins to exit to her bedroom.)* Miss Elizabeth, what's "Kitchen Mechanics Night?"

ELIZABETH. You don't know what that is?

HUSBAND. No, Ma'am.

ELIZABETH. When a colored woman cleans house, or cooks, or takes care of white folks children and she sleeps in their house ... what we call "sleeping in," we call them "Kitchen Mechanics." Thursday night is usually the night they have off. So on Thursday nights, the Savoy Ballroom let women ... colored women ... in for free up until eight o'clock and they call it "Kitchen Mechanics Night."

QUILLY. *(Offstage.)* Will you all please keep quiet out there! Shoot! *(Elizabeth exits to bedroom as lights go to black.)*

END OF SCENE

Scene 3

Time: 8:20, Friday morning.

At rise: Quilly is pacing in the living room. She crosses to the telephone and picks it up.

QUILLY. You on the telephone already? Don't you think we would like to use the telephone sometimes?... What do you mean wait until you're finished?... You're never finished.... Look, this is an emergency.... *(A key is heard in the door lock. Quilly hangs the telephone up as Elizabeth and Husband enter laughing.)* Where have you been?

ELIZABETH. Good morning, Quilly.

QUILLY. I've been worried sick about you. I didn't even go to work worrying about you. Where you been?

ELIZABETH. Let's talk about this in your room, Quilly.

QUILLY. No. This is my house. If anybody is going to leave the room, it's going to be him. *(To Husband.)* We would like some privacy if you don't mind.

HUSBAND. Yes, Ma'am. *(He crosses to the door to leave the apartment.)*

ELIZABETH. Where you going, Husband?

HUSBAND. I was going downstairs until....

ELIZABETH. You don't have to leave the house, Husband. You live here too. I know you must be just as sleepy as I am, so you go on in your room and lay down.

HUSBAND. Yes, Ma'am. *(He exits into his room. Quilly picks up the telephone receiver again and listens.)*

QUILLY. *(Screaming.)* Get off the doggone telephone! *(She slams the receiver back into the cradle.)* We're going to have to get rid of this party line and get a private line even if it does cost more money. I ain't used to all this party-line stuff, shoot. That cow is still on the telephone. I couldn't even call my white woman to tell her I wasn't coming in. If I could have gotten through, I was going to call the police about you.

ELIZABETH. Don't do that again, Quilly. I'm a grown woman. I'm not a child and I'm not your child, so don't be talking to me like one.

QUILLY. Well then, stop carrying on like one. *(Pause.)* I was worried about you. I didn't know if you were in the hospital or laying somewhere dead. I leave you sitting up at two-thirty in the morning ... with him, and then I wake up and you're gone. Your bed ain't been made or nothing. I knocked and knocked on his door ... no answer. I open the door and his bed ain't even been slept in! I didn't know what to think ... if you were dead or what. Why did you leave without telling me?

ELIZABETH. I don't have to get your permission to go out, Quilly!

QUILLY. At two-thirty in the morning?... and now it's almost eight-thirty?

ELIZABETH. We went out, we ate ...

QUILLY.   Where did you all go to eat, Frogmore?

ELIZABETH.   … we talked and laughed and I enjoyed myself.

QUILLY.   That wasn't right, Bess … to leave me to worry about you like that.

ELIZABETH.   After all these years, all of a sudden you're worried about me.

QUILLY.   I don't know what's gotten into you. God knows I don't. That geechee must have you fixed. I'm going to get myself ready for work. *(She exits to her bedroom. After a beat, Husband peeps out of his room, then enters. He is carrying his face cloth, towel, soap, toothbrush, toothpaste, razor and lather mug with brush.)*

HUSBAND.   I'm sorry if I caused you any trouble.

ELIZABETH.   You didn't cause me no trouble. I told you before, Quilly always has to be fussing about something. I'm going to lay down and get me some sleep.

HUSBAND.   Yeah, I'm sleepy too. *(He crosses to the opening leading to the bathroom, then stops.)* Miss Elizabeth?… I hope you don't mind me saying, but I sure enjoyed being with you last night.

ELIZABETH.   This morning.

HUSBAND.   Uh, yes, Ma'am … this morning.

ELIZABETH.   Well, thank you, Husband. I enjoyed being with you too. *(Awkward silence.)*

HUSBAND.   It's daytime, so I guess we can't say "good night," and "good day" just don't sound right.

ELIZABETH.   I ain't never been up all night to where I had to say "good night" in the daytime.

HUSBAND.   Me neither.

ELIZABETH.   Maybe we can just say, "sleep good."

HUSBAND.   Or as my mama used to say, "sweet dreams."

ELIZABETH.   All right, "sweet dreams."

HUSBAND.   *(Pause.)* My mama used to kiss me when she said that. *(Elizabeth and Husband stare at one another for a beat.)* I guess I'll go wash up. *(He exits to the bathroom. After a beat, there is a loud knocking on the door.)*

ELIZABETH.   Who is it?

LOU BESSIE.   It's Charmaine. I want to talk to Andre. *(Elizabeth crosses to the door and opens it. Lou Bessie enters.)*

ELIZABETH.   How did you get in the building?

LOU BESSIE.   Some fool came out and I just walked in. Now where's Andre?

ELIZABETH.   You mean, Husband.

LOU BESSIE.   Yeah, Husband. That's exactly who I mean. Now, where is he? *(Elizabeth crosses and calls down the hall.)*

ELIZABETH.   Husband!… Husband?

HUSBAND.   *(From offstage.)* Yes, Ma'am?

ELIZABETH.   Lou Bessie is here for you.

HUSBAND.   *(From offstage.)* I'll be right there, Miss Elizabeth.

ELIZABETH.   He'll be right out.

LOU BESSIE.   I heard. And I told you my name is Charmaine!

ELIZABETH.   I sure am going to try real hard to remember that. *(Husband enters from the bathroom pulling on his shirt.)*

HUSBAND.   Hey, Lou Bessie. I thought….

LOU BESSIE.   Don't give me that, "Hey, Lou Bessie" crap. You won that drawing for that breakfast because I took you to the Renaissance Ballroom. You've got some damn nerve taking some other woman out to eat a breakfast I won for you.

HUSBAND.   I paid for the ticket, Lou Bessie. Just like I paid for everything for you last night … and your friends. *(Quilly enters changed for work.)*

LOU BESSIE.   I don't give a damn what you paid. I took you there. If it wasn't for me, you would have never even bought the damn ticket. Then I got to hear from my friends about you coming into Whimpy's with some other woman … some "Old Settler" and eating breakfast at my expense. I'm out there trying to set things up for us and you're running around all hours of the night with some "Old Settler." As a matter of fact, they called her an "Old, Old, Settler," laughing their asses off.

ELIZABETH.   If you're going to use that kind of language, you can't talk in here.

LOU BESSIE.   I'll talk any way I want.

ELIZABETH.   Not in this house you won't.

LOU BESSIE.   Let's go in your room, Husband.

ELIZABETH.   I told Husband when he came here to rent, no drinking, no smoking, no cursing and no women allowed in the room.

LOU BESSIE.   What? *(To Husband.)* You mean you're paying rent for a room and you can't even have your own company in there?

ELIZABETH.   That's right. No women in the room.

LOU BESSIE.   I wasn't talking to you.

ELIZABETH.   Well, I was talking to you. No women in the room!

LOU BESSIE.   Well, I guess that includes you too ... doesn't it? *(There is a beat of silence.)*

HUSBAND.   Uh ... Lou Bessie....

LOU BESSIE.   I'm getting the hell out of here! *(She crosses to the door and exits.)*

ELIZABETH.   Good! And take your foul mouth with you.

HUSBAND.   Lou Bessie, wait.... *(He exits after Lou Bessie. We can hear them arguing outside the door for a beat.)*

QUILLY.   *(Pause.)* Well, I'm....

ELIZABETH.   I don't want to hear it, Quilly.

QUILLY.   I ain't got nothing to say about him and her or him and you. All I want to say is that I'm leaving for work. If my white woman calls looking for me, tell her I already left. I'll tell her that the subway broke down or something. She probably won't be able to get through anyway with motor-mouth on the telephone. *(She picks up the telephone and listens. Then screams into the telephone.)* Get off the phone! *(She slams the telephone down in the cradle. The front door opens and Husband enters, rushing to his room. After a beat, he exits his room with his jacket and hat in his hand. He crosses to the door, then stops.)*

HUSBAND.   I'm sorry about Lou Bessie, Miss Elizabeth. I ain't never heard her talk like that ... cursing and all. *(Pause.)* She has to go back to Great-Neck now. I'm going to take her to the train station ... try and calm her down. *(Pause.)* I'll be back. *(He starts to exit. Elizabeth crosses to her rocking chair, sits and begins to rock, looking out of the window.)*

ELIZABETH.   Husband?

HUSBAND.   Yes, Miss Elizabeth?

ELIZABETH.   Where does Lou Bessie live?

HUSBAND.   She lives out in Great-Neck.

ELIZABETH.   No, I mean when she's here in Harlem. When

she's not "sleeping in" out in Great Neck. *(Pause.)* She has to sleep somewhere.

HUSBAND. I don't rightly know, Miss Elizabeth.

ELIZABETH. Isn't that something you ought to know?

HUSBAND. I ain't never thought about it. *(Pause.)* Miss Elizabeth ... if you don't mind, I'd like to ask you a question.

ELIZABETH. What is it, Husband?

HUSBAND. *(Hesitantly.)* What's an "Old Settler?" *(There is a silence.)*

ELIZABETH. Quilly is better suited to answer that question.

QUILLY. *(Pause.)* An "Old Settler" is what folks up here call a woman pushing forty who hasn't been married and don't have any prospects. An "Old, Old Settler" is a woman....

HUSBAND. That's all right, Mrs. McGrath. I think I can figure that out for myself.

LOU BESSIE. *(From offstage.)* Andre! You coming? *(Husband exits.)*

QUILLY. *(Pause.)* What you said to that boy about where that woman lives, and what you just put on me to tell him, were two mean things to do, Bess. No matter how sorry I am, you're still going to rub my face in it. You'll never let me forget it. *(She exits as lights go to black.)*

END OF SCENE

Scene 4

Time: The same day, late afternoon.

At rise: Elizabeth enters the living room from the hallway carrying sheets, pillowcases and towels. As she crosses to Husband's room, the front door opens and Husband enters.

HUSBAND. Hi.

ELIZABETH. Hi. I was just fixing to change your sheets.

HUSBAND. I only slept on them three days. Besides, You

37

don't have to be doing that, Miss Elizabeth. If you just give me the sheets, I can change my own bed.

ELIZABETH.   It's part of what you get when you rent the room. But if you don't want me to go into your room....

HUSBAND.   Oh, no. It ain't nothing like that, Miss Elizabeth. It's just that I know how to do it. My mama made sure. She taught me to clean house, wash, iron, cook, everything. She used to say that I had to know how to do those things for myself in case I got tied up with one of those "lazy, good-for-nothing" women who's always complaining about how tired they were and didn't want to do nothing. *(Elizabeth gives the sheets, pillowcases and towels to Husband.)*

ELIZABETH.   All right. Here. Just put the dirty ones in the bathtub.

HUSBAND.   Yes, Ma'am. *(He begins to exit.)*

ELIZABETH.   It sure took you a long time to get home from Penn Station.

HUSBAND.   Yes, Ma'am. You see, when I got to that Penn Station with Lou Bessie, she was still put out with me. So ... she kind of made me ride with her to Great-Neck. She fussed all the way out there. People were just turning around and looking at us. I was sure glad when she got off that train.

ELIZABETH.   You mean to tell me, Lou Bessie made you ride all the way out to Great Neck and back?

HUSBAND.   Yes, Ma'am. Kind of.

ELIZABETH.   It still shouldn't have taken you this long.

HUSBAND.   Well, you see ... I kind of got lost. After Lou Bessie got off the train, I stayed on and ended up at the last stop ... a place called Port Washington. Then I didn't know which train to take to get back.

ELIZABETH.   You've got to get off the train and take another train back, Husband.

HUSBAND.   Yes, Ma'am. I sure know that now. *(Elizabeth begins to exit.)* Miss Elizabeth ... I'm sorry Lou Bessie called you that name.

ELIZABETH.   You can say it, Husband ... "Old Settler."

HUSBAND.   Yes, Ma'am. Well, I'm sorry.

ELIZABETH.   Did you tell her who the "Old Settler" was?

HUSBAND. No, Ma'am. I didn't want to cause you no more trouble on my account.

ELIZABETH. It don't matter none.

HUSBAND. It does to me. I don't know what's gotten into Lou Bessie. She never used to act like that....

ELIZABETH. I told you before, Husband, people change.

HUSBAND. I guess. But even I know that there's change for the good and change for the bad and the way I see it, Lou Bessie ain't changed for the good. *(Pause.)* Anyway, if you want me to move....

ELIZABETH. I ain't said nothing about you having to move, did I? Do you want to move?

HUSBAND. No, Ma'am. I was just thinking that maybe you didn't want Lou Bessie coming around.

ELIZABETH. I ain't studying no Lou Bessie. *(Pause.)* I'm fixing to get me something to eat. You eat anything since the restaurant?

HUSBAND. No, Ma'am.

ELIZABETH. You hungry?

HUSBAND. I sure wouldn't mind having something to eat, yes, Ma'am.

ELIZABETH. All we have right now are leftovers. That's what we have all week when it's Quilly's turn to cook. *(She crosses into the kitchen as Husband follows.)*

HUSBAND. Sometimes leftovers taste better than when you first cook them. The flavor has a longer time to settle in. *(Elizabeth and Husband stare at one another for a beat. Then Elizabeth crosses into the kitchen and begins to prepare the meal. Husband follows.)* Can I help do something?

ELIZABETH. No. You just sit down. There ain't nothing much to do. Besides, I ain't one of those "lazy, good-for-nothing women" your mama warned you about.

HUSBAND. I could tell that from reading your letters. I could see that from the beginning. *(Pause.)* Miss Elizabeth, I lied.

ELIZABETH. Lied about what?

HUSBAND. About not knowing where Lou Bessie lives when she's in Harlem.

ELIZABETH. I shouldn't have asked you that. It was mean

39

and unchristian. My way of getting back at Lou Bessie. You ain't got to tell me nothing.

HUSBAND. But I've got to say this, Miss Elizabeth.

ELIZABETH. It's not my business, Husband. And I don't want to talk about Lou Bessie.

HUSBAND. But it's important that I tell you.

ELIZABETH. Why?

HUSBAND. Because … because of the feelings I've been having even before I found Lou Bessie. The feelings I had when I used to read your letters and they said things to me that wasn't written on the paper. Because the same feelings were there when we were laughing and talking in that restaurant. And they were there, but in a different way, when Lou Bessie called you an "Old Settler." And they were there when she got off that train in Great-Neck and I didn't care that she was leaving; and that I couldn't wait to get back here.

ELIZABETH. Why did you feel you had to lie?

HUSBAND. I didn't want you to think that I was a fool or something. I already know Mrs. McGrath don't think that much of me. *(Pause.)* You see … Lou Bessie has a little three-year-old daughter that her Mama takes care of for her down in Frogmore. She had the baby by this man named Bucket....

ELIZABETH. Bucket?

HUSBAND. Yes, Ma'am, Bucket. I don't know why they call him that, but that's his name. Well, when he found out that Lou Bessie was pregnant, he took off. Now don't get me wrong, Lou Bessie ain't a bad person. She sends money down home for her little girl all the time. But she caught the devil from them people in Frogmore when they found out she was going to have a baby and wasn't married. But what really hurt her the most, was the way her mama treated her so mean. I sure felt sorry for her. So then after a while, I took up with Lou Bessie. Not because I felt sorry for her or nothing! I always had an eye for her, even when she was going with Bucket. Anyhow, Lou Bessie always claimed that she didn't know where Bucket had gone. So, last night when I finally got a chance to talk to Lou Bessie, I told her that I was going to come back here and get my things and move in with her.

40

ELIZABETH. You was planning to live common law?

HUSBAND. Yes, Ma'am. I know it would have been wrong. And I would have never done it if my mama was still living. But it was only going to be for a little while ... just until we got married.

ELIZABETH. I see.

HUSBAND. Yes, Ma'am.... So, anyway, that's when she told me that she was living with Bucket. She said that she couldn't afford to pay rent in a place that she was only sleeping in one or two nights a week, so she moved in with Bucket. But, Miss Elizabeth, Bucket only has a room ... one room ... like me. Only enough room for one bed like me. So, I asked her, "Where do you sleep, on the floor?" And she said that she sleeps in the same bed with Bucket, but that nothing's happening between them. I told her, "Here you are, sleeping in the same bed with the man you done had a baby by, in your night clothes, and you tell me nothing's happening?"

ELIZABETH. So, what she say?

HUSBAND. She told me I would just have to trust her.

ELIZABETH. Is that what she told you?

HUSBAND. Sure as I'm standing here.

ELIZABETH. Lord have mercy. That's a whole lot of trusting.

HUSBAND. To be honest with you, Miss Elizabeth, I kind of didn't care. Other than the fact that I didn't like her thinking I was some kind of fool, I found I didn't care. Now maybe if I had found her right off when I first got up here, things might have been different. But, I don't care.

ELIZABETH. Why not?

HUSBAND. I thought about that all the way back from Great-Neck and I figured it's because of those feelings I just finished talking about. *(Pause.)* Now, I don't mean no disrespect, Miss Elizabeth. I have all the respect in the world for you. Now, I know I'm kind of young and all, but I know my feelings. I know what makes me feel good and I suspect you know what makes you feel good. That's why we were able to stay up all night in that restaurant talking and laughing. You ever stay up all night with anyone before, Miss Elizabeth?

ELIZABETH. No.

41

HUSBAND. Me neither. Now, you see what I'm talking about? I know you had the same....

ELIZABETH. Husband, listen....

HUSBAND. Please ... don't stop my nerve now. I got my nerve up and I got to keep going, because if I stop, I may not be able to get up the nerve to start again. *(Pause.)* Now, all I want is to keep that feeling for as long as I can. So, I'm asking that you let me spend some more time with you like we did last night.

ELIZABETH. Don't play with me, Husband. I'm too old for that.

HUSBAND. Ain't no playing here, Miss Elizabeth. And you're not too old, you're just older. I had an uncle used to say, "There ain't no such thing as a woman that's too old or a woman that's too ugly. Only women that are not too nice."

ELIZABETH. What you want with me?

HUSBAND. I just want to feel good, the way you make me feel ... like in that restaurant ... like when I read your letters. *(He begins to move towards Elizabeth, who begins to retreat.)*

ELIZABETH. This ain't right. I told you, don't play with me.

HUSBAND. And I told you, I ain't playing. *(Elizabeth's retreat is halted by a wall.)*

ELIZABETH. What about Lou Bessie?

HUSBAND. You said you didn't want to talk about Lou Bessie ... neither do I. *(He has gotten very close to Elizabeth. He kisses her.)*

ELIZABETH. No, this ain't right. Why are you doing this?

HUSBAND. Because I want to and I believe you want me to. Now, come on to Husband. *(Elizabeth breaks away.)*

ELIZABETH. Go on now. *(Husband crosses to Elizabeth, taking her hand.)*

HUSBAND. I don't believe you want me to do that.

ELIZABETH. Go on now. *(Husband kisses Elizabeth again. This time she gives in.)* This ain't right. *(The lights go to black.)*

END OF ACT ONE

ACT TWO

Scene 1

Time: Saturday, two weeks later, mid-afternoon.

At rise: Elizabeth is sitting at the kitchen table sewing the sash of her dress and singing, "Didn't It Rain?"* She is wearing a robe and slippers, with a kerchief wrapped around her head.

ELIZABETH.
>Didn't it rain, children?
>Rain all night long?
>Didn't it?
>Woo!
>Didn't it?
>Woo!
>Didn't it ?
>Oh, my Lord, didn't it rain?
>
>Didn't it rain, children?
>Rain all night long?
>Didn't it?
>Woo!
>Didn't it?
>Woo!
>Didn't it?
>Oh, my Lord, didn't it rain?

(The front door opens and Quilly enters. She is carrying a box with three carnations [two white and one red].) Husband?... I ain't ready yet! You said....

QUILLY. You and Husband ain't the only ones living here ... just because you act like it.

ELIZABETH. Oh, Quilly. I thought you were at the church helping to set up for the Mother's Day Program.

* See Special Note on Songs and Recordings on copyright page.

(Singing.)

> Didn't it rain, children?
> Rain all night long?

QUILLY.   I haven't heard that song in years!

ELIZABETH.   Remember how we used to sing it in church when we were little?

(Singing.)

> Didn't it rain, children?
> Rain all night long?
> Didn't it?

Come on, Quilly! That's your part. *(Quilly enters the kitchen. She sets the box with the carnations in it on the table.)*

QUILLY.   Why did I always have to sing that part?

ELIZABETH.   Because the first time we sang it in church, you were three-years-old and that's all you knew how to sing. Remember? And the people just loved you. They thought you was the cutest thing. And you was.

QUILLY.   Yeah. Mama and Papa was proud of me. But every year the people wanted us to sing that same song. Here I am, seventeen-years-old, you singing all the words, and I'm just standing there saying, "woo, woo."

ELIZABETH.   That's because you were so good at it ... and cute. I bet to this day, you still don't know the words.

QUILLY.   Why should I? I never got a chance to sing them, shoot!

ELIZABETH.   Well, those were happy times for us and I'm happy now. So, do me a favor, just this one time, and sing it with me.

QUILLY.   No!

ELIZABETH.   Oh, come on, Quilly. Please, please, please....

QUILLY.   Okay, okay, just this one time to shut you up.

ELIZABETH.   Oh, thank you, Quilly. Thank you, thank you....

QUILLY.   Oh, shut up and sing.

ELIZABETH.   *(Singing.)*

> Didn't it rain, children?
> Rain all night long?
> Didn't it?

QUILLY. *(Singing.)*
    Woo!
ELIZABETH. *(Singing.)*
    Didn't it?
QUILLY. *(Singing.)*
    Woo!
ELIZABETH. *(Singing.)*
    Didn't it?
    Oh, my Lord, didn't it rain?

    Didn't it rain, children?
    Rain all night long?
    Didn't it?
(Quilly does not respond.) Didn't it?
QUILLY. What are we going to do, give a recital? Shoot. I don't feel like "wooing" no more. I've got to get ready to go back to church for the Program.
ELIZABETH. I thought you were serving Mother's Day dinner at Mrs. Rudusky's.
QUILLY. I ain't going. I'm going to go to the Mother's Day Program at the church and then I'm bringing my behind on home and putting it in the bed.
ELIZABETH. She's depending on you! You can't do that at the last minute!
QUILLY. Yes I can! I don't feel like being around no white folks today.
ELIZABETH. What's the matter with you?
QUILLY. You remember how Sister Wallace at the church was so happy because she and her four children was going down to Georgia to spend Mother's Day with her mama?
ELIZABETH. Yeah.
QUILLY. She hadn't seen her mama in six years. The poor woman had been saving all year to get the train fare. Me and some of the other people at the church even fried chicken and baked biscuits and cornbread and cake and put it in shoe boxes so they could have something to eat on the train. Well, they left last night. But when we got to church this morning,

Reverend Osborne told us that Sister Wallace had called his house crying. Seems when they got to Washington, DC, her and those children had to get out of the car they was sitting in and move back to the colored cars at the end of the train. But there was only two colored cars and all those colored folks couldn't fit in just those two cars. Now, those greedy crackers had done over-booked the whole train. So when white folks didn't have seats in the all white cars, the railroad would charge them half price if they would be willing to ride the colored car. And if they were, a colored person had to get up and let the cracker have their seat. If there were too many colored people standing in the aisle, they'd make some of them get off the train. They kept letting white folks on and kept kicking Negroes off until there was no room for Sister Wallace and those four children. So now she's stuck in Washington, DC, with a little bit of money and a couple of shoe boxes of fried chicken and cornbread.

ELIZABETH.   Lord have mercy. What's she going to do?

QUILLY.   How am I supposed to know? As of an hour ago, she and them children were still sitting in the colored waiting room. She's not going to make it to Georgia for Mother's Day, I know that. I don't know what make white folks so mean.

ELIZABETH.   Some of them sure are something. But, Quilly, you can't blame Mrs. Rudusky for that.

QUILLY.   Why can't I?

ELIZABETH.   Because she's been very good to you. We can't blame all white people for what some white people do. We don't want them to blame all Negroes for what a few of us do.

QUILLY.   They do don't they? *(The telephone rings.)* My goodness! Motor-mouth must have died. A call came through! *(She crosses to the telephone and answers it.)* Hello.... Oh ... yeah.... *(To Elizabeth.)* It's for you. *(Elizabeth crosses and takes the telephone from Quilly.)*

ELIZABETH.   *(Into telephone.)* Hello.... Oh, hi.... Yeah, I'm getting ready now.... No, I haven't changed my mind.... How late are you going to be?... What kind of surprise?... *(Laughing.)* No, tell me now.... *(Laughing.)* That ain't fair. I tell you what, you can tell me now and when you get here, I'll act as if it's a surprise that I know nothing about.... All right, but I still don't think it's fair.... What?... I can't now.... *(Laughs.)* Yeah, I do.... But, I can't now ... I just can't. Okay, I'll see you then. Bye. *(She hangs the receiver up. To Quilly.)* That was Husband.

QUILLY. No kidding.

ELIZABETH. I have to finish dressing. *(Quilly picks up the box with the carnations in and give it to Elizabeth.)*

QUILLY. Here. I got some Mother's Day carnations for us to wear. They don't look that good this year and they sure were high.

ELIZABETH. Thanks, Quilly. I forgot all about getting carnations for Mother's Day.

QUILLY. I can't imagine why. *(Indicating Husband's room.)* You see, I even bought one for him.

ELIZABETH. That's very thoughtful of you. But, remember, Husband's mother died a while back. He should wear a white carnation. You wear a red carnation when your mother is living and....

QUILLY. I know that. But that's all they had left. He ought to be thankful that I thought to buy him one at all. I don't care if it's red, white or orange and green striped! Shoot!

ELIZABETH. He didn't say nothing, Quilly. Don't get mad at him. All I said was that you wear white....

QUILLY. Then give him your carnation, shoot. Then you can go to the Mother's Day Program without one.

ELIZABETH. *(Pause.)* I'm not going to the Program.

QUILLY. You're getting dressed.

ELIZABETH. *(Hesitantly.)* Husband is taking me out to eat.

QUILLY. *(Pause.)* What's wrong with you, Bess?

ELIZABETH. There ain't nothing wrong with me. We're just going out to eat.

QUILLY. Okay. Why don't you bring him to the Program at church? That boy needs to go to church as confused as he is ... and that's the God's honest truth. Then after the Program go and eat. Or eat at the church, they're serving.

ELIZABETH. We can't. He's taking me somewhere special.

QUILLY. Where?

ELIZABETH. I don't know, it's a surprise.

QUILLY.   Old Husband is just full of surprises. One day he's really going to surprise you. You mark my word.

ELIZABETH.   I got to finish dressing. *(She exits to her bedroom.)*

QUILLY.   *(Calling offstage.)* He probably ain't taking you to eat nothing but a old pimp steak, shoot. We both know what this is all about, Bess. When you have a roomer, you don't cook for him. He's been eating here every night this week.

ELIZABETH.   *(From offstage.)* I've been buying extra and I've been cooking extra.

QUILLY.   Yeah, but has he been giving you extra? *(Pause.)* Or maybe he has.

ELIZABETH.   *(From offstage.)* That's a common thing to say, Quilly!

QUILLY.   This ain't got nothing to do with how much you buy or how much you cook. You're too old for that boy ... too old to be out there trying to pop your fingers ... acting like some of those old fast teen-age girls on the streets. Did you hear yourself on the telephone? *(Mimicking.)* "Hee, hee, hee, that ain't fair. Hee, hee, hee, I can't now." *(Pause.)* And what about Miss Lou Bessie Charmaine? Have you forgot about her? *(Elizabeth enters in a very stylish dress and high-heeled shoes. She is carrying a pocketbook, gloves and a hat. Her hair is done in a nice new style.)* My goodness gracious! Just going out to eat, huh?

ELIZABETH.   I ain't studying nothing you got to say, Quilly. Are my seams straight?

QUILLY.   Yeah, they're straight, but you need a girdle. Then again, forget it. Can't nothing else fit in that dress. *(Elizabeth crosses to the mirror to put on her hat.)* Did you hear what I was saying about.... *(A key is heard in the door. The door opens and Husband enters. He is dressed in a loud, colorful zoot suit with a wide-brimmed hat, chain and all.)*

HUSBAND.   Hello, everybody!

QUILLY.   Lord Jesus, help us please.

HUSBAND.   How do you like my surprise, Bess?

QUILLY.   Bess?

HUSBAND.   Bess said it was all right if I called her Bess.

QUILLY.   Then I guess it's all right.

HUSBAND.   *(Turning around.)* Well, how do I look?

48

QUILLY. Just like I said ... confused. You could kill a roach in a corner with the tip of those shoes. *(Husband takes off his hat revealing his newly processed hair [a conk]. There is silence.)*

HUSBAND. What's the matter?

ELIZABETH. I won't go out with you looking like that, Husband.

HUSBAND. What's wrong?

QUILLY. You look like a clown!

HUSBAND. This is what they're wearing. Every place I went with Lou Bessie, the hip cats were wearing this.

QUILLY. They would be if Lou Bessie took you. And what do you know about some "hip cats?"

ELIZABETH. Quilly, will you please be quiet! *(To Husband.)* The suit is bad enough, Husband, but why did you have to mess up your hair?

HUSBAND. Lou Bessie said....

ELIZABETH. *(Screaming.)* I don't want to hear no more about Lou Bessie! *(She exits to her bedroom.)*

QUILLY. *(Pause.)* Ain't no use you standing there looking like Uncle Ben before he started cooking rice.

HUSBAND. What did I do?

QUILLY. If you don't know, you need to go on back down in the woods with your old country self, because that's just where you belong. Because if you stay up here, that heifer, Lou Bessie, is going to get you killed or put in jail. And don't let the door knob hit you where the good Lord split you. *(Pause.)* Why ain't you in the Army with the rest of the boys your age?

HUSBAND. The Army ain't called me and I ain't going looking for them. I ain't going nowhere to get myself killed for folks who would kill me right here just for wearing the uniform ... no, Ma'am. I believe if they put me between one of those Japanese soldiers and one of those German soldiers and gave most white folks here a gun and told them to shoot, most of them would shoot me.

QUILLY. Looking like you look, I would too. What does Lou Bessie say?

HUSBAND. I ain't studying no Lou Bessie.

QUILLY. Oh, no? Who got you to conk your hair? Who

dressed you up like a clown? You think Bess wants to go any-place with you looking like a runaway from a minstrel show. You asked me what you did, well here's what I think. Used to be, any time things didn't go your way, your mama was there to wipe your tears. Now, Mama's gone and you're up here chasing after that old-lazy-good-for-nothing-somebody-of-a-woman and things ain't going right. So, you latch on to my sister ... the Old Settler ... old enough to be your mama, and you two fool each other into thinking it's love.

HUSBAND. I do love her! Mrs. McGrath, I don't know why you're so against me, but you don't have no cause to say something like that.

QUILLY. I got cause because that's my sister and I don't want her heart torn from her body. I've seen it done once thirty years ago ... maybe I could have done something about it and maybe not, but I don't want to see it done again.

HUSBAND. I don't mean Bess no harm.

QUILLY. I don't think you know what you mean. But I'll tell you this. It may not show. We may fuss a lot, but I love my sister very much. She's done a lot for me. She's all I got in the world. So, if you hurt her, I'll run over you like a truck over a rooster, and that's the God's honest truth. (Elizabeth enters changed into something more conservative.)

ELIZABETH. Come on, Quilly. We don't want to be late for the Program at church.

QUILLY. Don't forget the carnations. I've got to change. (Elizabeth gets the box with the carnations as Quilly exits through the hallway.)

ELIZABETH. Quilly thought to buy you a Mother's Day carnation. They didn't have three white ones, so you take this one. (She gives Husband a white carnation.) Quilly and I can share the other white one.

HUSBAND. Thank you.

ELIZABETH. Don't thank me, thank Quilly.

HUSBAND. I will then. (Pause.) Bess, I asked you when I first got up here, that if I did anything wrong, that I wanted you to say something or stop me ... and you promised you would. But now you got all put out with me and you won't tell me why.

ELIZABETH.   Look at how you did yourself, Husband. Look at what you did to your hair.

HUSBAND.   I was only trying to look good for you. Lou Bessie said I looked so bad. And I know I didn't look like those other fellows Lou Bessie knew....

ELIZABETH.   I'm not Lou Bessie. That's something you can't get through your head. Did I say you looked bad?

HUSBAND.   No, Ma'am.

ELIZABETH.   Did I tell you to cook up your hair like that?

HUSBAND.   No, Ma'am.

ELIZABETH.   *(Angered.)* Will you stop "No, Ma'aming" me! I'm supposed to be your woman, not your mama!

HUSBAND.   Yes, Ma'am ... I mean yes.

ELIZABETH.   Then why didn't you ask me, and not Lou Bessie, before you went and messed yourself up like that?

HUSBAND.   Because Lou Bessie said....

ELIZABETH.   This is a mistake ... and when you get to be my age, you can't be making too many mistakes. You got too much Lou Bessie on your mind.

HUSBAND.   Well, if you made a mistake, then me spending all of this money must be a mistake too.

ELIZABETH.   Don't be blaming buying them clothes on me.

HUSBAND.   I ain't talking about no clothes. *(He goes into his pocket and removes a ring case. He crosses and hands it to Elizabeth.)* I told you I had a surprise for you. *(Elizabeth takes the ring case and opens it.)*

ELIZABETH.   Ooooo ... Husband.

HUSBAND.   Well, go ahead and put it on. No, no, wait a minute. Let me do it. *(He takes the ring and puts it on Elizabeth's finger.)*

ELIZABETH.   *(Admiring the ring.)* It's so pretty.

HUSBAND.   You like it?

ELIZABETH.   I sure do.

HUSBAND.   *(Proudly.)* It costed me ninety-seven dollars at Busch's Jewelry store on 125th street. They told me I could pay for it with some money down and so much a week, but I just paid them outright.

ELIZABETH.   Quilly!... Quilly!... *(Quilly enters running in her*

"Ladies of the Golden Scepter" uniform. Her gloves, pocketbook and hat are in her hands. Elizabeth extends her hand to Quilly.) Quilly, look!

QUILLY. *(Pause.)* I suppose this means you're not going to the Mother's Day Program … again.

ELIZABETH. Quilly, please be happy for me.

QUILLY. You weren't happy for me. You didn't even speak to me for eight years.

ELIZABETH. That was different and you know it.… Please, Quilly. *(Quilly crosses to the mirror and puts on her hat. She then crosses to the door. She stops for a beat, then turns and crosses to Elizabeth and hugs her.)*

QUILLY. I am happy for you. *(Pause.)* I'm going to be late for the Program. *(Quilly crosses to the door and exits.)*

HUSBAND. What happened to cause you and Mrs. McGrath not to talk for eight years?

ELIZABETH. I'll get around to telling you about it at some point. Right now, I'm happy and I don't want to think about anything unhappy. And I'm ready to get something to eat.

HUSBAND. Me too.

ELIZABETH. And I don't want no pimp steak.

HUSBAND. Pimp steak? What's that?

ELIZABETH. You don't know what a pimp steak is? A hot dog!

HUSBAND. *(Laugh.)* That's a good one. *(Pause.)* I can't do nothing about my hair right now, but I'm going to change my clothes.

ELIZABETH. You can stay away from that Lou Bessie too.

HUSBAND. Yes, Ma'am … I mean, yes.

ELIZABETH. I'm going to change too. Bet I'll be ready before you.

HUSBAND. Bet you won't. *(Elizabeth turns and runs up the hallway. Husband exits into his room as the lights go to black.)*

END OF SCENE

Scene 2

Time: 9:30 A.M., Sunday, the next day.

At rise: Quilly is in the living room standing in front of the mirror putting on her hat. Elizabeth enters in slippers and robe with a kerchief on her head.

QUILLY. Happy Mother's Day.

ELIZABETH. I ain't nobody's mama.

QUILLY. You sure about that?

ELIZABETH. *(Sitting.)* Don't be starting no stuff with me the first thing this morning, Quilly. I ain't up to it. Can't get no sleep. Did you hear little Charles doing all that screaming? Delores must have been spanking him in the room right next to me. Sounded like he was right in my bedroom.

QUILLY. She should spank his little behind in every room in that apartment, as spoiled as that child is.

ELIZABETH. She don't have to spank him every day.

QUILLY. He's bad every day, ain't he? She wasn't doing nothing to that boy anyway ... and he over there screaming bloody murder. He ought to be mine. I'd set his little hind-pots on fire. He wouldn't be able to sit down for a week. That's right. Spare the rod and spoil the child. That's what's wrong with these kids today....

ELIZABETH. You sure shouldn't be going to no church this morning, as evil as you is.

QUILLY. At least I'm going, shoot. When's the last time you been? Not since that boy moved....

ELIZABETH. How did Sister Wallace and her children make out?

QUILLY. When I got to the Mother's Day Program last night, Reverend Osborne told us that, Sister Wallace and those children finally did get on another train. But it was the same thing ... only two cars for the colored folks. Say, the people was standing on top of one another in the aisles. Some people was sitting on their suitcases. They couldn't move ... couldn't even

53

turn around it was so tight. *(Proudly.)* But you know what happened, Bess? Say, the men who was sitting, all got up and turned the seats around so you had two seats facing one another. Then the men let the women and small children sit in three of the seats and a man sat in the fourth seat. And every half-hour, the man who was sitting, would get up and let a man who was standing take his seat. Some of the women wanted to take turns standing, but the men wouldn't hear it. No woman or child had to stand. I tell you, Bess, those colored men sure make me feel proud to be a Negro. I wanted to call some of the members this morning, but Miss-Mile-A-Minute-Mouth was at it again. You know we can ask the telephone company to put us on another line with somebody else. I guess I'll hear something more when I get to church.

ELIZABETH.   Why didn't you wake me up this morning in time to go?

QUILLY.   I barely got up myself. I didn't get to bed until after twelve and didn't get to sleep until after you came in ... which was about three. So I didn't think you would be able to get up and go to church.

ELIZABETH.   That sure enough is right. I've got the biggest headache. I had some champagne last night.

QUILLY.   Champagne? You don't drink. What you doing drinking champagne?

ELIZABETH.   We went to eat, then we went to the movie to see Herb Jeffries in, *The Bronze Buckaroo.* And then....

QUILLY.   That's an old movie.

ELIZABETH.   So what, Quilly? I hadn't seen it. Goodness! Then Husband took me to Small's Paradise where we had a glass of champagne to celebrate him giving me the ring.

QUILLY.   How he going to pay for that ring ... a dollar down and a dollar when they catch him? He ain't got no job.

ELIZABETH.   He paid for it outright. And he paid for the champagne outright. And we didn't eat no pimp steak.

QUILLY.   You stop going to church. You start wearing tight-fitting clothes. You start staying out half the night finger-popping and cutting the fool. You used to not drink, now you drink champagne and sit up in beer gardens. Soon all kinds of filth

54

will be coming out of your mouth just like that Lou Bessie. That's what you're doing ... trying to be a Lou Bessie for him.

ELIZABETH. Quilly, it was only one glass of champagne to celebrate.

QUILLY. Yeah, that's just like all those people who talk about only drinking to be sociable.

ELIZABETH. *(Getting up.)* If I wanted to hear preaching, I would be hurrying to get dressed so I could go to church with you. *(She crosses to exit into the hallway. She then turns and crosses back to Quilly.)* If you wasn't happy for me, why did you lie and hug me last night?

QUILLY. Because I wanted to be happy for you.

ELIZABETH. And?... And?

QUILLY. I've already missed Sunday School. I don't want to be late for church too.

ELIZABETH. It's not just that he's younger than I am.

QUILLY. Yeah, he's younger. He's walking a long ways behind you in age.

ELIZABETH. But, it's more than that, isn't it? *(Pause.)* What is it? *(Pause.)* If it was a man with a woman half his age, you wouldn't be making such a fuss, would you.

QUILLY. You're not a man ... and neither is he. That's a mama's boy looking for another mama and you fit the bill. Even that old cricket-brain Lou Bessie said that the first time she came here. Even she knew that. Lou Bessie ain't what the chickens left, but, as sad as it is, she's the woman in his life. You're just the new mama.

ELIZABETH. *(Holding up her finger.)* Who has the ring ... Lou Bessie or me?

QUILLY. Yeah, you got the ring, but did you get it the same way Lou Bessie gets what she wants from him?

ELIZABETH. What's that supposed to mean?

QUILLY. You know good and well what I'm talking about.

ELIZABETH. Let me get one thing straight. I told Husband that I don't believe in laying down with no man before marriage and he respects that.

QUILLY. What you going to do when that boy's nature get up, Bess? That's a young, healthy, strong, country boy. What you going to do when his nature gets up two and three times a night ... and day? You haven't used it in so long ... if you've ever used it at all, that you don't even know if it works. And if you can't cut the mustard, you're going to have to lick the jar.

ELIZABETH.   Why you got to be talking all up under people's clothes like that?

QUILLY.   Because it's life. You too old to have any babies.

ELIZABETH.   Don't you think he knows that?

QUILLY.   So, what's going to happen when he starts wanting a son? You think you're going to be like Abraham's wife Sarah in the Bible? You think God's going to touch your belly and out going to pop a little Husband?

ELIZABETH.   We've already talked about that I told you.

QUILLY.   It's one thing to talk about it, but it's another thing to be faced with it. When he gets the yearning and you keep saying you're too tired.... When he wants to continue his name and you can't provide him with a way to do that ... not even a daughter, that's where a Lou Bessie comes in.

ELIZABETH.   Oh, will you shut up! Shut up! Why are you so mean? I came up here and worked and sent Mama money so she could buy you shoes and clothes for school. When Mama died, I went down there and got you and brought you back up here to live with me. I fed you and put clothes on your back until you started working at a job I got for you. And after you tore my heart out and shamed me before the whole world, then didn't talk to me for eight years, I still loved you and swallowed my pride and came looking for you to make peace. Because you was my sister. We came out of the same body ... shared the same mother. Because there was nobody else in this whole world with the same blood as mine running through their veins, and it wasn't right for us not to be talking to each other ... loving each other. Because if I couldn't give you anything else, love was the one thing I could give you every day of my life ... and I tried. What terrible thing have I done to you ... other than love you, to make you treat me so mean? You hurt me.

QUILLY.   You're finally getting to it, ain't you, Bess?...

ELIZABETH.   … Stole from me!

QUILLY.   I couldn't have stolen what wasn't really yours.

ELIZABETH.   You knew I loved Herman and….

QUILLY.   But Herman didn't love you, Bess!

ELIZABETH.   He did until you came up here with your fast self!

QUILLY.   He didn't love you and he told you so. You just wouldn't listen like you won't listen now. He even told you that before I came up here … before he ever saw or knew me. Didn't he?

ELIZABETH.   That's why you know so much about Lou Bessie, because you was just like her.

QUILLY.   Didn't he?

ELIZABETH.   And then you want to flaunt that picture of you and him together in the house I took you into … again.

QUILLY.   Didn't he tell you he didn't love you? Tell the truth, Bess. You know he didn't love you.

ELIZABETH.   *(Screaming.) You was my sister! (Pause.)* It didn't matter if he loved me or not! You was my sister and you knew I loved him! That meant you should have kept your hands off. *(Pause.)* If you hadn't come along, I would have made him love me. Maybe that's why you're so against me and Husband. Maybe you're jealous and want him too. Well, this is one you're not going to get. We're going to leave here in a couple of weeks after we get all of our business taken care of. We're going to take the train to Elkton, Maryland and get married and then get back on the train and stop in Halifax, so I can take care of some more business then head on down to his place in Frogmore. So you'll only have to put up with Husband and me for two more weeks, then the place is yours … and you can put that picture of you and Herman anyplace you want. *(She begins to cross out of the room.)*

QUILLY.   You're going to leave me. You're going to leave me up here alone. *(Pause.)* You've known since we were little girls that I was always afraid of being alone. First it was you, me and Mama; then it was Mama and me; then Mama died and I came to live with you, then I married Herman and after Herman, I came back to live with you. I ain't never been alone. I don't know why, but I'm scared of being alone. I don't want to die alone.

ELIZABETH.   Quilly, you left me alone. After Mama died, the one thing I loved in the whole world, other than the Lord and you, was Herman, and you came up here and stole him away from me. And you never once said you was sorry. Never! *(After a beat of silence, Quilly turns and crosses to the door to exit, then stops.)*

QUILLY.   Maybe you'll feel better knowing that I didn't kick Herman out like I said. We're separated all right, but Herman walked away from me with the young girl from the apartment across the hall. I came home from an all day retreat with the Ladies of the Golden Scepter and they were gone. *(Elizabeth turns her back on Quilly. After a beat Quilly crosses back to Elizabeth.)* I know I've never said it, but, honest to God, I've tried to show it. I'm sorry for what I did to you, Bess. I'm truly sorry for the hurt. *(After a beat of no response from Elizabeth, Quilly exits.)*

ELIZABETH.   The good don't die alone, Quilly. God always sends someone from the other side to greet us. *(As the lights go to black, the sound of a song like "My Troubles Are So Hard to Bear,"* by Ethel Davenport, rises.)*

END OF SCENE

Scene 3

Time: Twelve days later.

In dark, we still hear a song like, "My Troubles Are So Hard to Bear,"* by Ethel Davenport, which is now coming from the radio.

At rise: Elizabeth is in the kitchen wrapping plates, cups and glasses in newspaper and putting them in a box which sits on the table. She hums along with the song. The telephone rings. Elizabeth crosses and answer it.

* See Special Note on Songs and Recordings on copyright page.

58

ELIZABETH.   *(Into telephone.)* Hello?... Hi!... Where are you?... Did you get the train tickets? How much did they cost?... Hold on, Honey.... Let me turn this radio off, I can hardly hear you. *(She puts the telephone down and crosses and turns off the radio. She then crosses back to the telephone continuing her conversation.)* Now, how much did they cost?... My goodness, that's high! What about the suitcases? Did you have any trouble getting them checked on the train?... The boxes are packed and ... oh, did you get your haircut yet? *(To the party-line.)* You've got some nerve cutting in on my call as much as you stay on the telephone ... I'll get off when I'm finished talking, that's when.... You're welcome very much.... *(To Husband on the phone.)* Don't she have some nerve? My goodness! Like I was saying, the boxes are packed and I have the other two suitcases.... *(There is a knock at the door.)* Lord have mercy! Hold on a minute, Honey, somebody's at the door. *(To the door.)* Who is it?
LOU BESSIE.   *(Offstage.)* Charmaine!
ELIZABETH.   *(To herself.)* Charmaine?... *(To door.)* Just a minute. *(Into telephone.)* It's Lou Bessie.... What's she coming by here for?... I thought you were supposed to stay away from her.... Why did you have to tell her? *(There is another knock at the door. To the door.)* Just a minute!
LOU BESSIE.   *(Offstage.)* I ain't got all day!
ELIZABETH.   *(Into telephone.)* Let me see what this woman wants. When will you be home? All right, call me in a hour ... I love you too. *(She hangs up the telephone and crosses to the door and opens it. Lou Bessie enters brushing right pass Elizabeth.)*
LOU BESSIE.   It sure took you a long time between "just a minute" and answering the door.
ELIZABETH.   How do you always get into the building without ringing the bell?
LOU BESSIE.   I ain't going to be standing in the street trying to catch no key in a handkerchief like some dog standing on his hind legs. I just stand there until someone comes out or is going in ... especially if it's a man. He sees a young — pretty thing ... like me, and he holds the door for her, no questions asked. But, you wouldn't know anything about that now would you?

59

ELIZABETH.   No, I suppose I wouldn't

LOU BESSIE.   See, it's called using what you got to get what you want.

ELIZABETH.   I reckon it....

LOU BESSIE.   Reckon? Reckon? I haven't heard that since I left from down home. Do you still say "over yonder?" I bet you still keep a slop-bucket under your bed.

ELIZABETH.   Just like you keep a "Bucket" in your bed. Right, Lou Bessie?

LOU BESSIE.   *(Pause.)* Going somewhere?

ELIZABETH.   You know good and well I am ... and Husband too.

LOU BESSIE.   I don't know no such thing. Because, you see, I didn't tell Husband he could go nowhere.

ELIZABETH.   I ain't going to let you and the devil take me to the outhouse today, Lou Bessie. So you just go on and say what you got to say then leave. *(She goes back to packing.)*

LOU BESSIE.   But you know what? On second thought, I do believe Husband did mention something ... in passing I mean ... about you and him going back down home to Frogmore. So, I'm going to do you a favor and give you some advice. You see, when Husband told me about you and him, you know what I did, huh, Bess?

ELIZABETH.   No, Lou Bessie. You tell me.

LOU BESSIE.   It's Charmaine — I laughed.

ELIZABETH.   Is that right?

LOU BESSIE.   I sure enough did. You think you're going to be Mrs. Elizabeth Witherspoon with your old self? Well, I don't care if it's "with-a-spoon" or "without-a-spoon," I can get him any time I want him. You won't be able to keep him.

ELIZABETH.   I won't try to "keep" him. I'll do my best to make him happy and love him as hard as I can. Then I'll pray that that will be enough for him to want to stay.

LOU BESSIE.   *(Laugh.)* You better do a whole lot of praying, especially in the mornings when he wakes up and sees what you look like laying next to him. *(Pause.)* You know how to take care of a man ... Bess? I'm talking about his needs ... not washing

60

his dirty draws. I bet if you had two minutes of loving and a cold glass of water, you'd drop dead. *(Laugh.)* Better yet, Husband says you ain't never been married. Have you ever had a man, Bess? No! *(Laugh.)* I bet you haven't! *(Laugh.)* Reminds me of something this cat told me over at Small's Paradise about this "Old Settler," who died, and had never had a man. They put on her headstone, "Who says you can't take it with you." *(Laugh.)* You know what I'm saying, Bess? See, I know how Husband is. *(Demonstratively.)* One foot in the east and one foot in the west and old Husband in the middle just doing his best.

ELIZABETH.   I'm sure you do know all about Husband and Jo Jo and Pee Wee and the Ink Spots....

LOU BESSIE.   I'd watch my mouth if I was you, Grandma.

ELIZABETH.   And you can go to hell.

LOU BESSIE.   Well, you can kiss....

ELIZABETH.   I know what you want, Lou Bessie

LOU BESSIE.   Charmaine!

ELIZABETH.   Lou Bessie! You don't want Husband, you want his money. But it ain't just that you'll take his money, you'll suck all the life out of him ... use him up. Then you'll leave him flat and empty. See, I know that you knew Husband was up here looking for you. You only came around when you heard that Husband had come into a piece of money. And that was the first thing that came out of your mouth ... what you was going to do with his money. Open a beauty salon/barber shop or some such thing ... move up to Sugar Hill or Striver's Row ... and with a friend to boot. Who's the friend, Lou Bessie?... The man you share the bed with ... telling Husband nothing's happening between the two of you.... Your little girl's daddy, Bucket?

LOU BESSIE.   You need to mind your old-ass business.

ELIZABETH.   I told you not to use that foul language in my house.

LOU BESSIE.   You just used it! You told me to go to hell!

ELIZABETH.   And I meant it too! Now, you get your hussy self out of my house.

LOU BESSIE.   I'm going, Old Settler. You ain't got to worry about that. But you remember what I told you.... *(Elizabeth starts to advance towards Lou Bessie.)*

ELIZABETH. Get out of my house.

LOU BESSIE. I can get Husband any time I.... *(Elizabeth is still advancing towards Lou Bessie as Lou Bessie backs to the door.)*

ELIZABETH. I told you to get out of my house.

LOU BESSIE. And you know what, Old Settler?... Just to show you I can, I'm going to take him. *(Elizabeth now rushes towards Lou Bessie.)*

ELIZABETH. Get out!... Get Out!... *(Lou Bessie turns and runs out of the apartment. Elizabeth stares at the closed door for a beat, then leans against it beaten. The sound of a song like "Troubles of the World,"* by Mahalia Jackson rises as the lights go to black.)*

END OF SCENE

Scene 4

Time: The same day, Friday, early evening.

Place: The living room of the apartment of Elizabeth Borny.

At rise: Quilly is sitting in a chair in the living room with a newspaper in her lap. She hears Elizabeth coming and picks up the newspaper as if she is reading. Elizabeth enters with two suitcases. She sets them down by the door.

ELIZABETH. Sister Oliver has recommended three women who are looking for a room. She said you can meet each one at the church tomorrow or they can come by here. You just have to let her know. *(Pause.)*

I've paid the rent for two months in advance. That will give you time to pick the woman you want to rent the room to without feeling rushed. *(She holds a receipt out to Quilly who does*

---

* See Special Note on Songs and Recordings on copyright page.

not respond. After a beat, she puts the receipt down on a table and exits back to the bedroom. After another beat, Elizabeth reenters carrying her coat, hat and pocketbook. She lays her coat across a chair and puts her hat on top of it.)

You won't have to go food shopping for at least a week. *(Elizabeth goes into her pocketbook and removes a piece of paper.)*

I'll be staying at Miss Mattie Welch's while I'm in Halifax. You probably don't remember her. She lives over by our church on route 301. I send her money to take care of Mama and Papa's graves.

QUILLY.   I know who she is.

ELIZABETH.   I wrote her address down. She doesn't have a telephone, but the telephone number is there for Mr. Sessom's General Store — if you might want to get in touch with me. *(Quilly still does not respond. Elizabeth puts the paper on the table next to the receipt.)*

Quilly, we've fussed and screamed about this. We've even said some things that sisters should never say to one another … and now we've barely talked to each other for almost two weeks … and I'm sorry for that. *(Pause.)*

Our family is almost over. There's only you and me left. I don't know how much time the good Lord has given us to share this earth, so I'm going to keep loving you. I know right now you don't like me, but I hope you still love me. But, I'm still going to leave with Husband tonight on that 9:20 train. And I would like to leave here knowing you're full of hope and good wishes for me like I would be for you. Now, any time you want to come down, you come on. Just like it was here, my door will always be open to you … my home will always be your home. *(She crosses to Quilly and kisses her on the forehead. Quilly gets up and exits to the bedroom. Calling after Quilly.)*

I'll come in and say good-bye before I leave. *(She now begins to move about the living room and kitchen, saying good-bye to the last thirty years. She crosses to the radio, turning it on. We hear a collage of different radio programs as Elizabeth paces about the apartment and sits in her rocking chair. The radio "signs-off " for the night. All is silent. The lights should begin to change indicating passage of time into early the next morning. At various stages during these changes,*

Elizabeth can be seen sitting, standing, pacing, etc. Occasionally, the sounds of approaching cars can be heard causing Elizabeth to look out of the window in anticipation. During the "passage of time," Quilly enters, unknowing to Elizabeth, and looks into the living room. Seeing Elizabeth now sitting and suffering, Quilly retreats into the kitchen where a special comes up on her as she suffers with Elizabeth in silence. She eventually sits at the kitchen table and doses off. When the morning "light" comes through the window, Elizabeth is seen still sitting in her rocking chair as if comatose. The radio "signs-on," waking Quilly. Quilly now enters the living room and turns the radio off. She then crosses to the lamp and turns it off. She now takes a chair and places it next to Elizabeth's rocking chair and sits looking out the window with her. Silence. A key is heard in the door lock. Husband enters carrying a bundle. Elizabeth and Quilly do not acknowledge him.)

HUSBAND. *(Breathless.)* Whew. I still had the keys. *(Pause.)*

Bess, I swear on my mama's grave I didn't mean to cause us to miss that train. I was on my way to that barber shop like you told me, but then I ran into Lou Bessie. *(Pause.)*

Uh.... She kind of knew I was going there because I told her when I called to say good-bye. She asked me to take some clothes with me down home that she had bought for her daughter. *(Pause.)*

Then ... I kind of ... stayed for a while ... and time kind of.... *(Elizabeth rises and picks up her coat, hat and pocketbook. She then crosses to the suitcases picking them up.)*

There's another train at 8:45 ... we can still catch it if we hurry. I already checked.... *(Husband attempts to assist Elizabeth who resists. She then exits up the hall to the bedrooms. After a beat, she reenters carrying the ring case.)*

ELIZABETH. Quilly — please? *(Quilly exits to her bedroom.)* I can't go with you, Husband....

HUSBAND. Bess....

ELIZABETH. No ... hear me out. You're a very good young man Husband, and I hope and pray that you become your own man and find the right path in life. Your mama would want the best for you and so do I. There's somebody out there who's right for you ... but it ain't me. All I can do is get in your way. I don't want that for you, and you shouldn't want that for you.

64

But, I truly thank you from the bottom of my heart for the last few weeks.

HUSBAND. Bess, nothing happened between me and....

ELIZABETH. It ain't that, Husband ... it's you and me. I just don't want to wake up one morning and look in your eyes and see that you want to be somewhere else ... with someone else. That would kill me. But I think your mama would appreciate me telling you that Lou Bessie ain't the right "someone else" either. Here now, you take this. *(She hands Husband the ring case. He doesn't take it. She pushes it gently into his hand.)*

Go on now. *(Husband takes the ring case.)*

Now I'm going to ask you to please go. *(She turns away and crosses to the rocking chair and sits. Husband turns to leave then turns back to Elizabeth.)*

HUSBAND. Bess, if you'll just give us....

QUILLY. *(Offstage.)* And leave the keys. *(Husband puts the keys down on a table and exits. Quilly enters. She crosses and stands behind the rocking chair. Pause.)*

We're still going to get that lock changed. We don't want no rapist walking in here, shoot. *(She looks out of the window.)*

Lord have mercy! You see the size of that needle that nurse got in her hand. Shoot, I wouldn't let nobody stick me with that. I don't know why they don't put some curtains or shades or something up to those windows.... They've got to know somebody's always looking. See, see, that man feels the same way I do. He ain't going to let that nurse stick him with that thing. *(Elizabeth rises and exits to the hallway. After a beat, she reenters carrying the picture of Quilly and Herman, which she places on the table among the other pictures. She then crosses to the couch and sits.)*

I'm going to call my white woman and tell her that I don't feel like cleaning her old dirty house today ... maybe not tomorrow either. I'm tired, shoot. *(Pause.)*

I didn't get a drop of sleep last night and it's my turn to cook this week. I sure don't feel like having no leftovers tonight, shoot. *(Quilly crosses to the couch and sits. Pause.)*

Let's go out and eat at Singleton's. I feel like having me some fried chicken ... the last part over the fence.... *(Quilly takes Elizabeth's hand.)*

Don't worry, I'll pay.... If you have to pay, all we'll have to eat are pimp steaks *(Laughs. Elizabeth's head falls over to rest on Quilly's shoulder as she begins to cry. Quilly puts her arms around Elizabeth's shoulders comforting her. There is a beat of silence. Then Quilly begins to hum, then sing. Singing slowly.)*

    Didn't it rain, children?
    Rain all night long?
    Didn't it?
    Woo!
    Didn't it?
    Woo!
    Didn't it?
    Oh my Lord, didn't it rain?

You never want to do the "Woo." Now you come on and do the "Woo."
(Singing.)

    Didn't it rain, children?
    Rain all night long?
    Didn't it?

(Pause.) Come on now, Bess! I've been "wooing" for fifty years. Now it's your turn to "woo."
(Singing.)

    Didn't it?

ELIZABETH.   *(Hesitantly.)*

    Woo.

QUILLY.   *(Singing.)*

    Didn't it?

ELIZABETH.   *(Hesitantly.)*

    Woo.

QUILLY.   *(Singing.)*

    Didn't it?

ELIZABETH and QUILLY.   *(Singing.)*

    Oh my Lord, didn't it rain?

(The lights begin to fade to black as Quilly and Elizabeth's voices segue into the voices of a gospel choir singing an upbeat version of, "Didn't It Rain."*)

END OF PLAY

PROPERTY LIST

Black pocketbook (ELIZABETH)
Black gloves (QUILLY)
Paper plate covered with wax paper (ELIZABETH)
White pocketbook (QUILLY)
White gloves (QUILLY)
Hand fan (QUILLY)
Key tied to a handkerchief (QUILLY)
2 cardboard suitcases, one tied with rope (HUSBAND)
Piece of paper (HUSBAND)
Sets of keys (ELIZABETH, HUSBAND)
Pictures (LOU BESSIE)
Glass of water (QUILLY)
Coupon (HUSBAND)
Face cloth (HUSBAND)
Towel (HUSBAND)
Soap (HUSBAND)
Toothpaste (HUSBAND)
Razor (HUSBAND)
Sheets (ELIZABETH)
Pillowcases (ELIZABETH)
Towels (ELIZABETH)
Box with 3 carnations (QUILLY)
Pocketbook (ELIZABETH)
Gloves (ELIZABETH)
Hat (ELIZABETH)
Ring case with ring (HUSDAND, ELIZABETH)
Cups (ELIZABETH)
Glasses (ELIZABETH)
Newspaper (ELIZABETH, QUILLY)
2 suitcases (ELIZABETH)
Receipt (ELIZABETH)
Piece of paper (ELIZABETH)
Picture (ELIZABETH)

AUTHOR'S NOTES

The songs that have been scripted work. It is not just the singing of the songs, but the mood and tempo in which they are sung:

> The song in ACT ONE, Scene 2, ("SATAN ... ") is sung very slowly and reflectively. ELIZABETH sings it having been transported into another time and place. She is unaware that HUSBAND is there until he joins in, at which time the tempo increases.

> The song at the beginning of ACT TWO ("DIDN'T IT RAIN?"), sung by ELIZABETH, is very up-tempo. However, QUILLY'S "woos" are dead, dry, and without enthusiasm.

> The song at the very end of the play (again, "DIDN'T IT RAIN?"), this time sung by QUILLY, is very slow tempo with a melancholy mood. It is very important that *both* sisters join to sing the last line of the song.

The songs are to be sung in the style of gospel singing of the time (1943), *sans* any vocal gymnastics. If there is no knowledge of the songs and how they should be sung, please contact the playwright or his agent. As of this printing, the author is living and can answer questions. The author kindly asks that directors add no other songs to the script.

It is 1943: The character of HUSBAND would not walk around the apartment with his shirt off in front of these two older women. Also, the women would not allow it. The character of HUSBAND would not sit in the living room in the presence of the women without being given permission. The character of HUSBAND would remove his hat when he enters the apartment, holding it in his hand.

The kiss at the end of ACT ONE is very innocent and very awkward. These are two people with no amorous experience to speak of. *They do not know how to kiss.* Add to that the taboo of a younger man with an older woman that existed in 1943. That alone should inform the kiss. They are not Scarlet O'Hara and Rhett Butler.

The silence in the last scene *works.* There is beauty in silence on stage — if directed properly. Please trust it.

NEW PLAYS

• **SMASH by Jeffrey Hatcher.** Based on the novel, AN UNSOCIAL SOCIALIST by George Bernard Shaw, the story centers on a millionaire Socialist who leaves his bride on their wedding day because he fears his passion for her will get in the way of his plans to overthrow the British government. *"SMASH is witty, cunning, intelligent, and skillful."* –Seattle Weekly. *"SMASH is a wonderfully high-style British comedy of manners that evokes the world of Shaw's high-minded heroes and heroines, but shaped by a post modern sensibility."* –Seattle Herald. [5M, 5W] ISBN: 0-8222-1553-5

• **PRIVATE EYES by Steven Dietz.** A comedy of suspicion in which nothing is ever quite what it seems. *"Steven Dietz's ... Pirandellian smooch to the mercurial nature of theatrical illusion and romantic truth, Dietz's spiraling structure and breathless pacing provide enough of an oxygen rush to revive any moribund audience member ... Dietz's mastery of playmaking ... is cause for kudos."* –The Village Voice. *"The cleverest and most artful piece presented at the 21st annual [Humana] festival was PRIVATE EYES by writer-director Steven Dietz."* –The Chicago Tribune. [3M, 2W] ISBN: 0-8222-1619-1

• **DIMLY PERCEIVED THREATS TO THE SYSTEM by Jon Klein.** Reality and fantasy overlap with hilarious results as this unforgettable family attempts to survive the nineties. *"Here's a play whose point about fractured families goes to the heart, mind -- and ears."* –The Washington Post. *" ... an end-of-the millennium comedy about a family on the verge of a nervous breakdown ... Trenchant and hilarious ... "* –The Baltimore Sun. [2M, 4W] ISBN: 0-8222-1677-9

• **HONOUR by Joanna Murray-Smith.** In a series of intense confrontations, a wife, husband, lover and daughter negotiate the forces of passion, lust, history, responsibility and honour. *"Tight, crackling dialogue (usually played out in punchy verbal duels) captures characters unable to deal with emotions ... Murray-Smith effectively places her characters in situations that strip away pretense."* –Variety. *"HONOUR might just capture a few honors of its own."* –Time Out Magazine. [1M, 3W] ISBN: 0-8222-1683-3

• **NINE ARMENIANS by Leslie Ayvazian.** A revealing portrait of three generations of an Armenian-American family. *" ... Ayvazian's obvious personal exploration ... is evocative, and her picture of an American Life colored nostalgically by an increasingly alien ethnic tradition, is persuasively embedded into a script of a certain supple grace ... "* –The NY Post. *"... NINE ARMENIANS is a warm, likable work that benefits from ... Ayvazian's clear-headed insight into the dynamics of a close-knit family ... "* –Variety. [5M, 5W] ISBN: 0-8222-1602-7

• **PSYCHOPATHIA SEXUALIS by John Patrick Shanley.** Fetishes and psychiatry abound in this scathing comedy about a man and his father's argyle socks. *"John Patrick Shanley's new play, PSYCHOPATHIA SEXUALIS is ... perfectly poised between daffy comedy and believable human neurosis which Shanley combines so well ... "* –The LA Times. *"John Patrick Shanley's PSYCHOPATHIA SEXUALIS is a salty boulevard comedy with a bittersweet theme ... "* –New York Magazine. *"A tour de force of witty, barbed dialogue."* –Variety. [3M, 2W] ISBN: 0-8222-1615-9

DRAMATISTS PLAY SERVICE, INC.
440 Park Avenue South, New York, NY 10016 212-683-8960 Fax 212-213-1539
postmaster@dramatists.com www.dramatists.com

NEW PLAYS

• **A QUESTION OF MERCY by David Rabe.** The Obie Award-winning playwright probes the sensitive and controversial issue of doctor-assisted suicide in the age of AIDS in this poignant drama. *"There are many devastating ironies in Mr. Rabe's beautifully considered, piercingly clear-eyed work ... "* –The NY Times. *"With unsettling candor and disturbing insight, the play arouses pity and understanding of a troubling subject ... Rabe's provocative tale is an affirmation of dignity that rings clear and true."* –Variety. [6M, 1W] ISBN: 0-8222-1643-4

• **A DOLL'S HOUSE by Henrik Ibsen, adapted by Frank McGuinness. Winner of the 1997 Tony Award for best revival.** *"New, raw, gut-twisting and gripping. Easily the hottest drama this season."* –USA Today. *"Bold, brilliant and alive."* –The Wall Street Journal. *"A thunderclap of an evening that takes your breath away."* –Time. *"The stuff of Broadway legend."* –Associated Press. [4M, 4W, 2 boys] ISBN: 0-8222-1636-1

• **THE WAITING ROOM by Lisa Loomer.** Three women from different centuries meet in a doctor's waiting room in this dark comedy about the timeless quest for beauty -- and its cost. *"... THE WAITING ROOM ... is a bold, risky melange of conflicting elements that is ... terrifically moving ... There's no resisting the fierce emotional pull of the play."* – The NY Times. *" ... one of the high points of this year's Off-Broadway season ... THE WAITING ROOM is well worth a visit."* –Back Stage. [7M, 4W, flexible casting] ISBN: 0-8222-1594-2

• **MR. PETERS' CONNECTIONS by Arthur Miller.** Mr. Miller describes the protagonist as existing in a dream-like state when the mind is "freed to roam from real memories to conjectures, from trivialities to tragic insights, from terror of death to glorying in one's being alive." With this memory play, the Tony Award and Pulitzer Prize-winner reaffirms his stature as the world's foremost dramatist. *" ... a cross between Joycean stream-of-consciousness and Strindberg's dream plays, sweetened with a dose of William Saroyan's philosophical whimsy ... CONNECTIONS is most intriguing ... Miller scholars will surely find many connections of their own to make between this work and the author's earlier plays."* –The NY Times. [5M, 3W] ISBN: 0-8222-1687-6

• **THE STEWARD OF CHRISTENDOM by Sebastian Barry.** A freely imagined portrait of the author's great-grandfather, the last Chief Superintendent of the Dublin Metropolitan Police. *"MAGNIFICENT ... the cool, elegiac eye of James Joyce's THE DEAD; the bleak absurdity of Samuel Beckett's lost, primal characters; the cosmic anger of KING LEAR ..."* –The NY Times. *"Sebastian Barry's compassionate imaging of an ancestor he never knew is among the most poignant onstage displays of humanity in recent memory."* –Variety. [5M, 4W] ISBN: 0-8222-1609-4

• **SYMPATHETIC MAGIC by Lanford Wilson. Winner of the 1997 Obie for best play.** The mysteries of the universe, and of human and artistic creation, are explored in this award-winning play. *"Lanford Wilson's idiosyncratic SYMPATHETIC MAGIC is his BEST PLAY YET ... the rare play you WANT ... chock-full of ideas, incidents, witty or poetic lines, scientific and philosophical argument ... you'll find your intellectual faculties racing."* – New York Magazine. *"The script is like a fully notated score, next to which most new plays are cursory lead sheets."* –The Village Voice. [5M, 3W] ISBN: 0-8222-1630-2

DRAMATISTS PLAY SERVICE, INC.
440 Park Avenue South, New York, NY 10016 212-683-8960 Fax 212-213-1539
postmaster@dramatists.com www.dramatists.com